Research Strategies

Research Strategies

Finding Your Way Through the Information Fog

Second Edition

William B. Badke

iUniverse, Inc.
New York Lincoln Shanghai

Research Strategies
Finding Your Way Through the Information Fog

iUniverse books may be ordered through booksellers or by contacting:

iUniverse
2021 Pine Lake Road, Suite 100
Lincoln, NE 68512
www.iuniverse.com
1-800-Authors (1-800-288-4677)

This book is a substantial revision of The Survivor's Guide to Library Research (Grand Rapids: Zondervan Publishing House, 1990). Zondervan is a division of HarperCollins.

ISBN-13: 978-0-595-31371-6 (pbk)
ISBN-13: 978-0-595-76186-9 (ebk)
ISBN-10: 0-595-31371-X (pbk)
ISBN-10: 0-595-76186-0 (ebk)

Printed in the United States of America

Contents

Preface

Everyone does research.

Some just do it better than others.

This book is definitely for you if you are:

❖ A university student whose term papers are patented as a cure for insomnia;

❖ A Dilbert of industry who's been told to do a feasibility study on the expansion potential of ice cream bar sales in Nome, Alaska;

❖ a simple honest citizen trying to find the truth behind the advertising so that the next car you buy won't be like your last one that made you *persona non grata* at the automobile association.

Are you ready for your next research project? Really ready? Do you have the skills and strategies to get the job done efficiently and effectively without panic attacks and the need for a long vacation when you're done? Do you have confidence that you can start with a topic about which you know nothing and end with an understanding of it that is neither trite nor superficial? Are you prepared to enjoy the experience? [Yes, I did say "enjoy."]

If the previous paragraph has left you feeling somewhat queasy, this book is for you. Even if you have significant research skills, you can learn better ones if you take the time to read on.

You have the privilege of living in the information age, with a zillion opportunities all around you to find out anything about anything. But faced with a humongous number of Internet sites, not to mention library databases of increasing size and complexity, knowing how to navigate through the information fog isn't something you can pick up easily on your own. Yet you can hardly call yourself educated if you don't know how to handle information systems and do research effectively, not in a world in which most careers are built on what you know or can find out.

Getting back to my earlier use of the word "enjoy," learning how to do research does not have to be painful. It can be fun. Honestly. Personally, research gives me so much pleasure that my family has to kidnap me out of the library whenever they want to go on an outing or buy groceries. You can have the same joy that I have. Read on.

1

Taking Charge

You may be saying to yourself, "I've never been good at this. In fact, I don't think I have a good research project in me."

My response is, "Of course you don't. A good research project is out there, not inside you. What you have to do is get out there, find the data, work with it, and make it your own."

Now, before you run off to a dark alley frequented by black market sellers of data, let me offer you a safer alternative. What follows is a list of basic things that you need to have working for you in order to turn your anxiety into a brilliant project, leading to an excellent product.

1. You need an intense desire to do a brilliant project, not just an average one. By definition, most people can do an average project.

2. You need to take your time and plan your research as a *strategy* rather than as a mad dash through libraries and databases. Libraries know when you have reached the panic stage. The books close ranks and refuse to be found. Titles in the catalog trade places so that you can't locate them. The smell of musty books renders you numb and silly. Databases can do even worse things to you (don't ask).

    Never panic. Take it easy. Work out a plan and show that data who's in charge here.

3. You need to become a friend to structure. If you're the kind of person who might follow your schedule if you could remember where you put it, or someone who views a library overdue fine as a reasonable price to pay for never having to think about a due date, research is going to be a battle for you. Structure and organization, from the beginning of the process all the way to its triumphant end, is crucial, no matter how much pain it will cost you to change your ways.

4. You need to develop *lateral thinking*. Lateral thinking is akin to what happens in a football game: The quarterback has no openings at all. If he runs with the ball, he'll be flattened. So, instead of moving forward, he throws the ball sideways to another player who can move it forward. These are the steps:

   ❖ Recognize that your advance along one line is blocked.
   ❖ Abandon your approach and look for another that is completely different.
   ❖ Run with your new approach and make it work (or try yet another).

It's like the old story of the truck that got stuck in a highway underpass. No towing vehicle of any kind could get it out, and so the workers were left with the option of dismantling an expensive truck or tearing down an even more expensive underpass until…

   …until the light bulb went on and some bright lateral thinker suggested letting the air out of the truck's tires to *lower* it.

Lateral thinking works beyond the obvious, in the realm of the creative. Nurture this gift within you. It will help greatly in that moment when all your cherished strategies have failed you and you still don't have the information you need.

Here's an example: Suppose you were doing research on the trials of Galileo and discovered that every book with the texts of the verdicts against him was already signed out. Rather than thinking that the library has let you down and you are doomed to wander the streets as a pathetic warning to others, think beyond the library (a lateral) and check to see if someone has posted the verdict transcripts on the Internet (they have—**http://www.law.umkc.edu/faculty/projects/ftrials/**

galileo/galileo.html). That's the sort of thinking that can save you from the disaster that often lurks, ready to bite the unsuspecting.

Wrestling with a Topic

"I'm writing a history paper on the Lollards. I don't know who they were (and I'm finding it hard to care). When I'm done—if I can find anything in this confusing yet undersized library—I will have a research paper describing the Lollards. It will stress description of the Lollards. Its theme will be 'Describing the Lollards.' The point I will seek to make is that the Lollards can indeed be described."

Exciting, isn't it? Don't those old Lollards just thrill you to pieces? Not really. It's just another research project, as tedious as the last one you did. *Fact is, it isn't even research.*

"What?" you say. "Not research? I searched the library catalog and periodical indexes and even the Internet, and I've got a ton of stuff here. Don't tell me I'm not doing research."

All right, I won't. Go ahead and write your paper and describe your Lollards. Turn it in and wait for your professor to read the thing and give you the usual dreary mark. Obviously, you don't like your prof anyway, and that's why you keep doing this too him or her. Professors are no strangers to the kinds of boredom you inflict on them. In fact they're almost used to the tedious task of marking your essays. You bore the professor, and the professor pays you back by giving you a C. Any illusion that you actually did research will be dead by the time you get the essay back.

Not wanting to be harsh without providing some help, let me ask: What is genuine research if it's not what you've been passing off? Let's begin by looking at what it is not.

Elements of False Research

➤ False research assumes that the task is to gather data and synthesize it. Thus the typical student "research" project involves amassing data, reading and absorbing it, then regurgitating it back onto a fresh piece of paper (sorry for the disgusting image).

➢ False research deals in generalities and surveys. It loves a superficial look at a big topic, and it abhors depth and analysis.

➢ False research asks no analytical questions and makes no pretense at advancing knowledge. It is content to report on what has already been done, to summarize the past.

➢ False research is so boring that you should be surprised it ever gets completed, let alone foisted on the longsuffering professor.

The Key to Genuine Research

What's the point of doing research? A flip response might be that a professor or employer told you to do a research project, and you're just following orders. But that's not the answer I'm looking for.

Consider this dilemma as an example: A few years ago you bought a car that was a disaster. Its maker should have been executed for delusions of adequacy. While most cars have water dripping out of the exhaust pipe, yours had lemonade. You spent so much time pushing it that you were able to qualify for a weightlifting competition at the next Olympics. Your mechanic added a new wing onto his house with the money you spent keeping it on the road. Now you're due for a new vehicle, and you are not about to be stung again. So what to you do?

Research!!

You pick up every consumer reporting and car testing book or magazine you can find. You talk to your friends. You go on the Internet. Why? Because you have a burning question to answer, and somewhere out there is the data you need to answer it.

This is what research is all about. The key to genuine research is *a good question*. Without a question, nothing you are doing can be called research. Just as your search through car books is driven by the query, "Which car should I buy this time?" so any research project worthy of its name is driven by a single research question.

What constitutes a good question? Here the situation becomes a bit more complex, because you need to begin rethinking the whole research process.

Later in this chapter, we will consider the actual strategies involved in getting a topic ready for research, but for now we need an overview of the basic principles. The first of these is that most any research project presented to you needs some work before it is viable enough to use.

Assume, first of all, that the topic is probably too broad to be workable unless you're planning to write a book. A topic like the Lollards or abortion or economic conditions in Russia today is not likely to inspire depth of analysis because you don't have space in ten or twenty pages to deal with anything but the superficial. You are going to have to focus on a more narrow aspect of the topic so that you can deal with it in depth. Consider a bathtub with a gallon of water in it as opposed to a bathroom sink with a gallon of water in it. Which is deeper? The sink, because its borders are narrower. The same principle works in a research project—the narrower your focus, the more chance you have of getting some depth into your project.

Assume, second, that you are going to have to develop a sound working knowledge of the topic before you're going to know what to do with it.

Assume, third, that you may have to have to negotiate with the one who gave you the project. You need to know that what you propose is actually going to fly with the person ultimately responsible for your fate. But cheer up—professors are generally thrilled with some tiny evidence of creativity in their students. Go to your professor and ask politely, "Would you mind if I pursued *this* issue raised by the Lollards? It looks really interesting."

Your professor's heart will turn to mush and he or she will say quietly, "Yes, all right," while inside he or she is shouting, "A new approach! I'm getting a new approach!"

Caution: Don't ever say, "May I write on the Albigenses instead?" This signals the professor that you don't like the Lollards, and you most certainly will end up having to write on the Lollards anyway.

A Model for Research

What, then, is research all about? Here's a model:

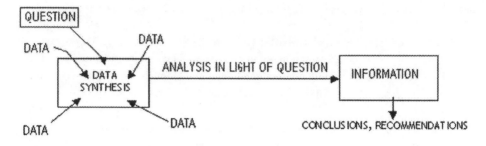

Explanation? You begin with a question, you collect data, you synthesize it, you analyze it in light of the question (leading to information), and then you come up with conclusions and recommendations.

The key to the whole thing is that you need to move beyond merely gathering data, reorganizing it (data synthesis) and reporting on what you read. When a question is injected into the mix, the data becomes more than an end in itself and turns into the raw material needed to answer the question. The result is analysis that turns data into information that can then be used to reach an answer.

Look's easy, doesn't it? Maybe it doesn't look easy at all to you, but we are about to embark on a journey that will make things much clearer.

Getting Started in Research

Getting a Working Knowledge through Reference Sources

Before you go off in all directions at once (like a draw-and-quarter competition at the local jousting match), get a grip on yourself. As I librarian, I see the same painful experience repeated day after day—students walking fearfully into our book stacks area, then stopping, frozen to the ground.

I know what's buzzing through their battered minds—"I'm here, I'm actually here in the library, about to start researching my topic, and I don't have a *clue* what to do. Time has stopped, and people are staring at me. Why can't I move my limbs? Why is my head so numb? Maybe I'll die here, rooted to the floor, and they'll bronze me as a monument to the unknown student."

Take heart—it doesn't have to be like this. Let me give you the first step you need to take in any research project, so that you break free from bondage. It's simple—*Get a working knowledge of your topic.*

Right, so what's a working knowledge? Here's a basic definition: *You have a working knowledge of a topic when you can talk about it for one minute without repeating yourself.*

To start your research, all you need to do is acquire one minute's knowledge. "One minute?" you say. "I've been told I have to present a fifteen page research paper with a dozen footnotes including appropriate periodical literature (whatever that is). Why talk to me about one minute of working knowledge?"

You need a working knowledge for the same reason that you take a flashlight with you when you have to stumble around in the dark. A working knowledge gives you the basics of a topic, enough light so that you won't hurt yourself as you move on into more complicated territory. It isn't complete knowledge, but it's enough to tell you what the topic entails, what its boundaries are, even what some of its controversies, mysteries and dangers might be.

So where do you get a working knowledge? You could simply go on the Internet, where virtually anything is explained by some site or other. But, if you don't know much about the topic to begin with, the Net may be a dubious source. How will you be able to tell that the information is reliable? (We'll cover that issue in Chapter Five).

You would do better to investigate authoritative *reference sources* first. All academic libraries have recognized reference tools that provide short, concise and authoritative information on virtually any topic you might think of.

Reference books will generally appear in the form of dictionaries or encyclopedias on general or specific topics. As well, handbooks, atlases—in fact, any tool that involves looking up brief information—may be found in a reference collection. Increasingly, reference sources are also appearing in electronic form, allowing for greater flexibility in searching. But you (or your library) will need to subscribe with real money to the best of these. The best reference sources are not available without cost on the Internet, though some older or lite versions of reference tools are appearing there for free.

So you're wondering how to find a reference book that will give you information on marriage customs of the Kurdish people. You could wander the shelves of the reference collection, but there's an easier way to find what you want. *Think of the broad subject within which you topic lies.* In this case, you are looking at customs of a particular culture. Thus you could look up in your library's catalog a subject heading like MANNERS AND CUSTOMS—ENCYCLOPEDIAS to find a reference Source like *Worldmark Encyclopedia of Cultures and Daily Life.* Then just look up "Kurds."

Let's try another example of the sort of material you're looking for in a working knowledge. You've been longing to find out who the Lollards were (or are), admit it. Let me give you a clue—they were a group of religious people who flourished in the late Middle Ages and early Reformation period. What sort of a reference source would you use for Lollards? How about a dictionary of church history? If you check into a couple of such dictionaries, following the famous 5 W's of inquiry, you might discover the following:

Who?

The Lollards were followers of John Wycliffe; more generally, the term was used of any serious critic of the English church in the late Middle Ages. Key figures in the movement were Nicholas of Hereford, William Swinderby, and John Purvey.

What?

Their teachings, summed up by the Twelve Conclusions of 1395, included personal faith, divine election, and the Bible as the sole authority in religion. They demanded that every person have the individual right to read and interpret the Bible.

Where?

The movement existed primarily in England and Scotland.

When?

It began in the 1380s (AD) and went underground after 1431 due to persecution. The movement declined in the mid-1400s but revived about 1490. It figured prominently in the congregational dissent of the seventeenth century and the rise of the Hussites in Bohemia.

Why?

The Lollards claimed to be a reaction to the control over human life and spirituality exercised by the Church of the time.

My two reference sources (*Oxford Dictionary of the Christian Church* and *New International Dictionary of the Christian Church*) also yielded a combined bibliography of over 15 sources on the Lollards.

Have I convinced you of the need for a working knowledge? If not, I hope you have lots of luck in your research—You're going to need it. Unless you start with a working knowledge you will inevitably founder the moment you reach deeper waters.

Finding a Good Question

Research is not research until you have focused it around a solid research question. But how do you come up with a question that is going to work?

1. **Narrow your Topic** to one aspect of it. A big reason why research can fail is that the researcher is trying to conquer the world with one project. You simply cannot cover all of the topic of teen suicide or abortion or the causes of World War One or how Martha Stewart can do what she does and still be only one person. You have to choose an aspect that is distinct enough that you can really work with it.

2. **Identify Controversies or Questions** related to your narrowed approach. There's no point re-describing what has already been described. To tell me once more who the Lollards were is to do what every reference source on the subject has already done. This is where those excruciatingly boring and superficial "research" papers come from. You must vow never to write another one. Find something worth investigating. In the case of the Lollards, you might want to focus on one Lollard (narrowing) such as Nicholas of Hereford, and discover what elements of his approach were effective putting forward his Lollard position (which will lead to the research question).

The broader your focus, the more shallow your paper. Avoid questions that survey large amounts of data. They will lead to bibliographies that deal with a wide variety of issues and papers that never dwell on any one thing for more than a few lines. Instead of looking at all the causes of WWI, find a crucial cause and analyze it. Narrow is good; big sweeping questions breed ugliness.

Research Questions—The Bad and the Ugly

Some research questions simply won't work. They are doomed to failure and will produce research projects that are walking disasters, if they can walk at all. One way to recognize a good question is to know what the bad and ugly ones look like, so here are some examples:

1. The Question that Isn't There—Imagine the horror of someone reading your "research" paper and looking desperately but in vain for a question, only to discover that there is none. What's the purpose of your paper—to tell me something I could have read in any reference book? To tell me once again what everyone knows already? To bore me with your knowledge of trivia?

2. The Fuzzy Question—Sure, there's a question, but it isn't defined or focused enough to make it possible to answer. Asking something like, "*Why was Saddam the way he was?*" is no help at all. What way *was* he? Are you talking about his role as dictator of Iraq, his use of chemical weapons, his oil strategy, or just what? Until you clarify your focus, you will find no

way to answer your question without simply surveying his whole history (something that would likely depress the life out of you).

3. The Multi-part Question—*You must never let more than one research question intrude into a research project.* The shotgun approach is out. Research identifies *one* question, deals with that question through analytical use of data, and *then quits.* Never *ever* get stuck in the kind of proposal that says, "This paper will deal with _____. I will also attempt to _____ and to_____ and to _____." Your second and third questions are loose torpedoes on your own ship. They will sink you because they'll kill your focus. One question per research project is all you need or want.

4. The Question that Will Not Fly—Some questions are amazingly inventive, but try to answer questions that the data simply will not answer. Asking *"What is the effect of the growth of the Internet on the prevalence of schizophrenia in the American population"* may look cool, but exactly how would you gather relevant data to answer it? If your question is ambitious, ask yourself whether or not it's possible to find an answer. If not, curb your enthusiasm.

[For more on research questions, including more examples of both the good and the bad, see the APPENDIX.]

The Preliminary Outline

Chances are, if you are indeed like other people, that you are not in any mood at this point to start thinking about an outline for your project. People who start working on their outline before they've done their first catalog search are either sick or lost souls, because any sensible person knows that you compose your outline AFTER you write your paper.

Wrong. If you want to spare yourself a ton of grief, start on an outline now. Why? Simply because you need to build yourself as clear a road map as possible in order to do your research efficiently (by "efficiently," I mean that you will save time). A research question may be crucial to give your searching a goal, but an outline is crucial to tell you in detail what you need to search for to reach that goal.

What's a preliminary outline? It is simply 3 to 5 points that you need to cover in order to answer the research question. You may change it over time, but you need to start on it now.

How do you develop a preliminary outline? Start with your research question. Suppose you have the following question: *Did Saddam Hussein have weapons of mass destruction when the Iraq War of 2003 began?* The question itself gives clues for a preliminary outline. You need to look at evidence that he did have such weapons, evidence that he didn't and possibly some explanation of where the weapons went if he did have them.

Once you have a few basic elements, try to organize them into a rough order. For example:

> The Evidence that Saddam had weapons of mass destruction
> Evidence that he may not have had such weapons
> > His protests of innocence
> > Lack of success in finding such weapons
> Possible explanation of where these weapons may have gone if he did have them

(With my luck, all sorts of weapons will be found by the time you read this, and my terrific question will be worthless.)

Your preliminary outline is just that—preliminary. You can change it and develop it at will, or even scrap it and create a new one. But you need to start on your outline as soon as you have a research question, because the outline tells you what you need to cover in order to write the paper that answers your research question.

How About a Few Good Examples?

"The Thought of Erasmus of Rotterdam"

Your much beloved philosophy professor has assigned you "The Thought of Erasmus of Rotterdam." Having studied a few philosophy dictionaries, you narrow your topic to "The Humanism of Erasmus of Rotterdam." You *could*, at this point, decide to begin your paper with "Erasmus of Rotterdam was born in the year…" You *could* go on to explain what he taught about humanism and then conclude, "It is clear that Erasmus was an important person who deserves more attention."

This method is called "regurgitating your sources." It establishes a conduit between your books and your writing hand without ever really engaging your brain. It also makes for a very dull paper. Professors fall asleep over dull papers.

On the other hand, you could be analytical. Having read your sources and affixed your working knowledge firmly in your mind, you could engage your brain in finding a research question. How about asking this: "What is the essential difference between the humanism of Erasmus and that of the modern *Humanist Manifestos I and II*?" This would certainly demand study of Erasmus, but it would go further.

Now your have the makings of an approach that could contribute something fresh and exciting to the topic.

"Homelessness in our Cities"

You are taking a sociology class and are supposed to write a paper on "Homelessness in our Cities." You could regurgitate some statistics, recite a few case studies and conclude, "It is obvious that we need to take action on this issue." Or you might narrow your topic and ask a research question like this one: "Do programs that arrest homeless teens and compel them to accept social worker assistance actually reduce the incidence of teen homelessness in the long run?"

"The Causes of the Ecological Crisis"

For a course on environmental issues, you have been assigned, "The Causes of the Ecological Crisis." You narrow this to focus on the human values in society that can lead to ecological problems.

A descriptive paper would string together quotations from current leaders in the debate who are decrying our attitudes of wastefulness and greed. Your conclusion could read, "Thus it is clear that we must change our attitudes." You have narrowed your topic, but you've failed to apply a research question to it.

An analytical research paper would go further, perhaps considering the common view that the western Protestant ethic, with its desire for dominion over the earth, is at the heart of the environmental trouble we are in. Your research question could be, "Is western Protestantism responsible for the environmental crisis?"

"Behaviorism as a Model for Social Engineering"

You have been given a topic which is fairly narrow but still covers a lot of territory. Why not narrow it down to the behavioristic model of B.F. Skinner? You might now take the easy way and summarize his book *Walden Two* as Skinner's model for social engineering (but easy is the way that leads to destruction).

Or you could ask how Skinner's model in *Walden Two* might need to be revised if basic human depravity were taken into account (something Skinner seemed blissfully unaware of).

➤ One final note of caution: *Always clear your narrowed-down topic and brilliant research question with your professor or supervisor.* Disaster could be awaiting you if you don't.

Of course, some of us *like* to flirt with disaster. Do you feel lucky?

For Further Study

Study Guide

1. What three things do you need to seek if you want to do research well?
2. Name four elements of "false research." Why is each an enemy of true research?
3. Define a "working knowledge" of your topic and explain why it's important to have one.
4. What is a "reference source?"
5. What are the steps to finding a good research question?
6. Formulate a definition for genuine research.
7. Describe the following types of bad research questions: The fuzzy question, the multi-part question, the big sweep, the question that will not fly.

Practice with Research Questions

Try out the following for yourself, determining whether each question is a good one or an bad one. Then check the suggested key below.

1. Did Martin Luther write anything criticizing the Jews?
2. What effect does homelessness have on the price of beds?
3. What's happening with Bill Gates now that he's made all that money?
4. Is there evidence that changes in emphasis in the children's welfare program in your area are the result of pressure from the press?
5. What happened in Iraq in 2003?
6. How could the looting of the museums in Iraq in 2003 have been avoided?

7. What are the main features of Fetal Alcohol Syndrome and what can be done both to treat and prevent this condition? Should all alcohol containers carry a warning?
8. What are the ethical implications of human cloning?

Suggested Key to Practice with Research Questions

1. Bad Question: Anyone with the works of Luther available can find the answer in less than half an hour. A research question is more than discovery of a fact. It has to deal with an issue that can be analyzed in depth.

2. Bad Question: This question is the never-will-fly variety. Even if there is some connection between homelessness and the price of beds, there is no conceivable way for you to find out the nature and extent of the connection. Sometimes two ideas simply have no obvious connection or the connection is such that no amount of searching will help you find out what it was. A similar sort of question might be one like this: *What has been the influence of early Twentieth Century liberal theology on morality in the United States?* Presumably there could well be an influence, but I can think of no survey or statistical tool that would give you an answer. The key to avoiding these kinds of questions is to ask yourself—Is there a reasonable hope that I can gather evidence that will lead to an answer? If there seems to be no hope, drop the question.

3. Bad Question: The point is a cloudy fuzz, not a point at all. What are you trying to discover?—What Bill Gates does with his day? Whether he's enjoying his money? Whether he should be spending it in other ways? As long as your question doesn't indicate a point or a direction you have no idea how to develop your paper. Here's a good focused research question to replace it: *How well has Bill Gates done proportionally to other young rich men in giving to charitable causes?* Now you know that your interest is going to be in investigating his charitable giving and that of his peers to see how well Bill's giving has gone. There's a point to it and evidence that can be found with a little digging.

4. Good Question: Why? It demands research and analysis and there is evidence available to support that research. What you would need to do is to discover when various complaints about this office were prominent in the press, then see whether or not changes in the office consistently followed periods of complaint.

5. Bad Question: This could be question in which the point is not defined (i.e. What is it about Iraq in 2003 that you want to investigate?) or is easily answered (answer = a war). In any case, I have no idea what direction to take this one. It must be defined better.

6. Good Question: It should be possible to look, in hindsight, at what happened and show what protections could have been devised to prevent the looting. Considerable writing has been done on the issue, so there should be lots of information.

7. Bad Question: This is your classic multi-point question. With this many points to answer, you will find that your project is cut up into a number of smaller projects, with no overall unity. Follow this rule—every research project must deal with only one issue.

8. Somewhat Good Question: There's a lot to research and analyze but you may well find that you run into far too many ethical implications to deal with. To solve this, limit your scope. For example, ask something like this: In dealing with human cloning, what are its ethical implications for our understanding of what a human being is?

Assignment for a Research Project of Your Own

1. Choose a topic of interest to you.
2. Get basic information about your topic from at least two specialised reference sources (not general encyclopaedias but subject specialized reference sources like *Dictionary of Developmental & Educational Psychology*) to get a working knowledge of it.
3. Summarise in about half a page what you've learned (your working knowledge), *listing the reference sources you used.* [NOTE: If you could not find a suitable reference source, use an introductory chapter from a recent book. **Established reference books either in print or in electronic versions are preferred, however.**]
4. List 4-5 possible research questions, in question form, related to the topic that might be suitable for an essay on the topic. These questions should deal with one aspect of the topic, as narrowly as possible. They should not be easy to answer, nor should they be intended to describe what is already known. Try to make them as analytical as you can.

2

Databases

There was a time when dinosaurs roamed the earth and every library had a card catalog. Things were easier then. To find a book, you had one of three options—look up an author, look up a title, or look up a subject heading. Research may be much more complicated now, but your power to search has multiplied because of the computer.

The Next Stage

Once you have a working knowledge of your topic and a sound research question (only *one* research question, remember?), you need to move on to more substantial materials, most often to books in libraries. Why go there first rather than to magazines or journals or the Internet? For several reasons:

❖ Books represent the established knowledge concerning a topic, while journal articles and Internet lean toward more experimental knowledge.

❖ Books tend to cover the topic more comprehensively, while journal articles look at far more narrow aspects of the topic.

❖ Books, as we will see in the next chapter, are dandy resources for further bibliography.

So how do you find books? One source of useful book titles has already made itself available to you—most articles in reference books have at the end of them a bibliography of key works on the topic. Make use of this resource.

Beyond that, you will need to search a library catalog. These days, this likely means that you will be using a computer.

It would be great if I could present to you one version of a computerized library catalog and say, "Learn how to use this, and you can do a search for books in any library in the world." But the fact is that there are dozens of different computer catalog programs around, and each uses a different set of search techniques.

Far better, for your purposes, would be an explanation of databases and how they work. Armed with this information, you can face any threatening computer catalog with courage and skill. So on to databases!

Database Searching

Chances are, you fancy yourself as a computer genius and the word "database" doesn't sound like "root canal." But that doesn't mean you've learned how to *search* a database quickly and efficiently, coming up with exactly the results you need most of the time.

Then again, you might not yet have warmed to computers, as if they were friendly creatures ever ready to help you, like a big Saint Bernard on a ski slope. For you, "database" may well be a bad word, a frightening word. If this is your situation let me provide you with a soothing message: "Fear not."

Actually, databases are everywhere, and I guarantee you've already searched one or more though not necessarily with all the skill you needed. When was the last time you used a phone book, a dictionary, a library catalog (even in card format)? All of these are databases. Here's a definition:

A database is any collection of data that can be retrieved using organized search procedures.

Phone books are databases of names, addresses and phone numbers. They are set up alphabetically, so that we can use an *organized search procedure.* involving the alphabet, to help us retrieve the data we need. (NOTE: Just to confuse us, the Yellow Pages are organized by subject, then by alphabet).

Most common print databases are easy to search. But when databases are in computerized form, a whole new set of problems emerges:

1. Computer databases are generally much larger than print ones.

2. There are few common conventions for searching computerized databases, so every new database is a new experience.

3. Unlike a phone book or a library catalog in card format, you can't really browse a computer database well. It's a black hole into which you are calling: "Please send me the information I want!" Computers, being inherently unintelligent, don't always understand what you want, and thus frustration sets in quickly. If you use the wrong search technique or terminology, the blessed machine may tell you that the data isn't in there when you know full well that it is.

Many people today are hotshots on computers. They can make the keys sing, the mouse roar and the CPU toast. But not many people today understand database searching well enough to do it efficiently.

Case in point—I once found the dregs of a search on a computerized periodical index database. The database itself had over 1,000,000 journal article citations listed in it, and this searcher had typed in the keyword *Johnson*, resulting in 4,386 hits. That is, 4,386 journal citations with the name *Johnson* had become available to him/her. What was worse, the searcher had actually started pulling up each of those 4,386 entries in turn, looking for the right one. Ten hours later, red-eyed, fingers like angry claws…one can only imagine the angst that this session built up.

You may know how to use a computer, but disaster will befall you if you don't understand how to search databases. Worry not, however. You are about to learn a few things.

The big problem with computer databases is not with getting information into them, but with *retrieving* the information you need. For this purpose, there are two basic search tools available to you: ***controlled vocabularies*** and ***keywords***. Let's look at each in turn.

Controlled Vocabularies

They sound nasty, but you're actually quite familiar with them already if you've done much work in a library. The most common controlled vocabulary in all of North America is the *Library of Congress Subject Headings* system, used in libraries. Let's take that as a model.

How did these subject headings originate? Quite simply, the Library of Congress (LC) in Washington, DC predetermined the terms by which most things in the world would be called and then organized these terms in alphabetical lists. Some subject headings were easy: dogs are **DOGS**, sunflowers are **SUNFLOWERS**, and so on. Some were more difficult: What do you call senior citizens? LC chose **AGED**, much to the outrage of senior citizens. Television faith healers are **HEALERS IN MASS MEDIA**. Why? *Because LC said so.* That's the point with controlled vocabularies. These vocabularies are created by people "out there" who then *control* them and refuse to allow you to change them. Thus:

Rule #1: *With controlled vocabularies, you have to use the subject terms provided by the system. You might not like the terms chosen, but they are all you've got. No variations are allowed; you have to use the subject headings in the forms provided to you.*

How does a controlled vocabulary work? Armed with a set of predetermined subject headings, catalogers decide which one (or more) heading to assign to a particular chunk of data. In the case of LC, every time they get a book to catalog, they write a description of the book (i.e. the catalog record) which then becomes data, and to that data is added one or more controlled subject headings. So a book entitled *Them TV Preachers* may have the subject heading **HEALERS IN MASS MEDIA** attached to it. A book called *Active Seniors in Today's World* may be labeled with the subject heading **AGED**.

Note something very important here. The book *Them TV Preachers* did not have any of the actual words of the subject heading in its title. The title told you the book was about TV preachers. It said nothing about healers or about mass media. The same was true for the second title—*Active Seniors in Today's World*— the term "aged" is not to be seen anywhere in the title. Why, then, were they given the subject headings they received? *Because some intelligent librarian sat down with these books, determined what they were about, and then assigned the closest subject headings from the already existing controlled vocabulary list.* Thus:

<u>Rule #2</u>: *The actual wording of the data record (book title or catalog entry) is not important for controlled vocabularies. Subject headings are assigned on the basis of somebody's judgment as to what the data is about.*

Consider the advantages: I have 5 books with the following titles:

> *Terminal Choices*　　　*Choosing Life or Death*
> *Euthanasia*　　　　　　*The Practice of Death*
> *The Right to Die*

All of them are about mercy killing or euthanasia. You might not have guessed that fact by looking at the titles, but the intelligent LC librarian has looked over these books determined that they are all about the same topic and assigned them all the same subject heading: **EUTHANASIA**.

Controlled vocabularies are a good solution to the problem of *retrieval*. How do we ask the right question so that the database will deliver to us the information we need? If we wanted a list of books about euthanasia, it would be nice to have a search tool that would enable us simply to type a predetermined word or phrase into the computer and get back a list of all the euthanasia books regardless of the wordings of the actual book titles. This is what a *controlled vocabulary* is designed for. Most of the books on euthanasia in a library will be retrieved just by typing in the subject term **EUTHANASIA**.

<u>Rule #3</u>: *Use a controlled vocabulary as a search tool when you want a collection of data on the same subject regardless of what the data actually says about itself.*

But let's be clear about one thing—controlled vocabularies are "controlled" in the sense that someone other than you has determined what they will be. You as the user can't mess with them by changing their words or combining them in strange ways. You *use* controlled vocabularies; you don't create them and you can't fool with their form.

<u>Rule #4</u>: *Messing with controlled vocabulary wording or form is strictly forbidden. Subject headings are created by someone other than you, and they can't be manipulated or turned into keywords.*

Just before we leave *LC Subject Headings*, let's see how this controlled vocabulary system works. The Library of Congress provides subject headings for its own books, but it has also conveniently issued its list of approved headings so that all of us can use their system. Most libraries in North America have chosen to do just that, so that your library's subject headings are likely derived from the Library of Congress.

Your library should have a print edition of *Library of Congress Subject Headings* as a set of large red volumes. Below is a typical page from the guide. On the right are the subject headings or alternative headings. On the left is a description of what you are seeing on the right. If you have trouble distinguishing left from right, look for italics (left) or non-italics (right):

LC authorized subject heading (bold print) -->	**Peanuts**
	[QK495.L52 (Botany)]
Library of Congress Class numbers for peanuts ->	[SB351.P3 (Culture)]
	UF Arachides
UF = "use for". These are terms	Arachis hypogea
which LC does not use or authorize.	Earth nuts
If you looked up "Earth nuts" in LC	Goobers
Subject Headings, it would say:	Grass nuts
USE Peanuts.	Ground-nuts
	Groundnuts
(Bet you never knew peanuts could	Monkey nuts
called so many things. "Goobers?")	Pindars
	Pindas
	Pinders
BT = "broader term." Peanuts	BT Arachis
are a subdivision of these.	Oilseed plants
RT = "related term"	RT Cookery (Peanuts)
NT = "narrower term"	NT Peanut products
	—Breeding
These are subdivisions of	—Irrigation
"peanuts." There's even one	—Law and legislation
subdivision of a subdivision:	—Storage
Peanuts—Storage—Diseases	— Diseases and injuries
and injuries.	

The Library of Congress has also provided a free version of its subject heading system online. While not as extensive as the print edition, it can be a handy way to identify an authorized subject heading. Here's how it works (with the usual disclaimer that everything may be utterly different by the time you read this):

Go to **http://authorities.loc.gov/**and click on "Search Authorities." On the next screen, make sure you have "Subject Authority Headings" selected, then type in what you think the subject heading should be. For example, you might type in "mercy killing." When you click on "Begin Search," the next screen will give you a list with maroon colored buttons on the left. If the button opposite the term you searched says, "Authorized Heading," then you know you've identified a proper subject heading. If it says "References," it's not an authorized heading, but clicking on the button will tell you what the proper heading is.

NOTE—*This index is not a library catalog in itself.* It is simply a computerized guide to subject headings that you can then take to a catalog and use to find the books you need.

Here are other types of computer databases in which you may find controlled vocabularies:

1.   Some periodical indexes (see chapter 4 for definition) offer the possibility of a "subject heading" or "subject alphabetical" search. Beware, however: the subject heading terms may not be the same as those used by LC. To offer some assistance, you may find a *thesaurus*, either as a link in the index itself or as a printed document near the computer terminal. This is a subject heading list for that particular index. If the *thesaurus* is right in the index, you can likely type in a word or two and be directed to the proper subject heading to use. Sometimes a *thesaurus* will be described as a "subject browse" function, but it will do the same task.

2.   The ERIC database (see chapter 5 for explanation—it's available on the Internet at **http://www.eric.ed.gov**) offers the possibility of searching by keyword or by "descriptor." A descriptor is a controlled vocabulary term. ERIC suggests that to find out what descriptors they use you should consult their electronic *Thesaurus* or locate a relevant document by keyword, then note down on or more of the descriptors used with the data you recover. After that, you can search by those descriptor terms to find other resources on the same topic.

Many databases today, including most of those on the Internet, can be searched only by keyword. As we will see, keywords have distinct advantages, but the lack of a controlled vocabulary search option can be a definite drawback when all you want is a set of data on one subject regardless of what the data says about itself.

Keywords

Controlled vocabularies are subject terms created and administered by real human beings. That's civilization. Keywords represent the Wild West of database searching—bold and exciting, but risky as can be.

Before we go much further, you need to recognize that controlled vocabularies and keywords are *radically different from one another* in form and content. Controlled vocabularies are created by people other than you, and their form can't be messed with. Keywords are created by you and offer a lot of scope for manipulation.

Every database is made up of words. Computers, though inherently unintelligent when it comes to real thinking, are experts at recognizing words. To understand how keyword searching works, you need to know that every time a new book is added to a library, it is cataloged by creating a *catalog record,* which might look something like this:

Title: Digital borderlands : cultural studies of identity and interactivity on the Internet/edited by Johan Fornäs...[et al.].
Author: Fornäs, Johan, 1952-
Publisher: New York : Peter Lang, c2002
Description: 196 p. : ill. ; 23 cm.
ISBN: 082045740X (pbk. : alk. paper)
Series: Digital formations ; v. 6
Subjects: Internet—Social aspects.
       Internet users.
       Group identity.
Bibliography: Includes bibliographical references and index.

Call No.: HM567 .D54 2002

In that one *record* is all the data that the cataloger has provided about that book. With this information, the computer will allow you to search for *significant words* in that record. Now, imagine that there are thousands of records, and you're interested in finding a list of books about the social ramifications of the Internet. You should be able to think of important words (= *keywords*) and input them as a computer search. The computer will then look for those words in each of the records in the database and will download to your screen any records that have the words you've asked for. In this case, your search might look like this:

Interact and Internet*

(Don't worry about the search form yet. We'll get to the details below).

You will get records for books with titles like:

- *Social consequences of Internet use: access, involvement and interaction*
- *Digital borderlands : cultural studies of identity and interactivity on the Internet*
- *Murder on the Net : a guide to logging on and using the Internet via an interactive murder mystery adventure*

(All of the above are real titles of real books)

Notice one little trick I performed—*TRUNCATION* (sometimes called *WILDCARDS*). In many keyword searches, you can type part of a word, then add an asterisk (*) or sometimes a question mark (?), and the computer will look for every word that begins with the letters you typed. E.g. **interact*** will ask the computer to search for **interact, interacting, interaction**, even **interactivity**.

You can also sometimes do **forward truncation** in which the asterisk goes at the beginning (rare) or **middle truncation**, in which truncation is done within a word (e.g. Wom*n)

Even given the variations allowed through truncation, keyword searching demands as much precision as controlled vocabulary searching. The computer will only find the exact thing you want it to find. If you mistakenly type **intract*** instead of **interact***, the computer will give you data with words **intractable**, thus spoiling your whole day and making you grouchy in social environments.

<u>Rule #1:</u> *With keyword searching, what you type is what you get. The computer cannot interpret your request or give you the next best solution. All it can do is identify the words you ask for and give you the relevant data. Garbage in, garbage out.*

Boolean Searching

Many years before computers, a man named George Boole invented a mathematical system that enabled people to visualize the combination of various classes of things. The computer people have taken his system into the world of database searching in order to formulate searches where two or more terms are used. Let's look at some of the basic commands used in Boolean searching:

The OR Command

Suppose that I'm looking in a database for information about cars. I realize that a keyword search will pull out all information that has the word "cars" in it, but some people use the term "automobiles." How can I tell the computer to look for *both* words at the same time and give me data whether that data uses the word "cars" *or* the word "automobiles?"

In a situation in which I am searching for synonyms—different words that mean the same thing—I use the OR command. Let's visualize it this way:

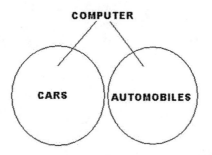

That is, "Computer, please give me everything on cars or automobiles, I don't care which." So you will get all the data with "cars" in it, plus all the data with "automobiles" in it.

In a keyword search in a computer catalog or some other database, your search may look like this:

cars or automobiles

Another situation calling for an **OR** search might be that in which two concepts are closely related, and you suspect that finding data on either of them will further your overall goal. For example, in doing a search for "psychoanalysis" you might also want to search for the father of psychoanalysis—Sigmund Freud. If you leave off the "Sigmund" (because he is usually referred to just as "Freud"), you can formulate a search like this:

psychoanalysis or Freud

With an **OR** search, you typically get a lot of "hits", that is, pieces of data brought down to you out of the database.

<u>Rule #2:</u> *An OR search is usually for synonyms or for keywords that are already closely related. You use it to anticipate the various ways something might be described or approached so that you don't have to do multiple individual word searches.*

The AND Command

One of the most profitable uses of keywords is in combining topics to narrow down a search. For example, a *Library of Congress Subject Heading* might lead you to something fairly narrow like **"Homeless Youth."** But what if you wanted to look at the problem of educating homeless youth? A subject heading search will probably let you down, *but a keyword search is just the ticket.*

Let's visualize it with a diagram first. If you're searching for the relationship between homeless youth and education, you don't want every piece of data on homeless youth, nor do you want every piece of data about education. You want the data that comes from having homeless youth and education intersect. Thus:

Your formulated keyword search will look like this:

homeless youth and education

A little tip: Be very careful not to add unnecessary words to AND searches. Suppose that you were searching for material in a database on Osama bin Laden's influence in the Iraq War of 2003. The temptation might be to load up your search with terminology, along the lines of:

Osama bin Laden and Iraq War and 2003 and influence

But stop and think (a nasty exercise, yet required occasionally)—You are searching for *keywords*, likely in a title. Are all these words likely to appear in a title, along the lines of "The Influence of Osama bin Laden in the Iraq War of 2003?" What about a title that goes along the lines of "Bin Laden and the Iraq War?" It's on target as far as your search goals are concerned, but your multi-word search above is going to eliminate this article from the result list. Why? Because the article does not have the words **Osama** and **influence**, nor the date **2003**, in its title. In other words, you eliminated a good article by demanding that too much terminology appear in each result you get.

How do you solve a problem like this? By becoming a minimalist:

Rule #3: *In an AND search, always look for the fewest number of terms required to get data that is on target with your search goals. The more unnecessary terms you add, the more you risk screening out good data that does not use those terms.*

For the search above, all you really need is:

Bin Laden and Iraq War

Hey, you might even be able to get rid of **Bin**. The "2003" isn't needed either, because Bin Laden wasn't involved in the 1990 Iraq war.

Back to our homeless youth—Keyword searching relates only to words actually in the data you're searching. If you think about it, "youth" could as easily be described as "adolescents," and "education" could be described with words like "school" and "schooling." Unless you enjoy doing many searches, you can do it all in one search by combining **AND** with **OR**:

Homeless AND (youth or adolescen*) AND (education or school*)

Notice that I put parentheses around the OR terms that belong together, because computer programs can get confused easily. The parentheses make it clear to the computer what to search. Notice as well that I truncated adolescen* to hit "adolescent" and "adolescence" and "adolescents." I also truncated "school" to cover "schools" and "schooling."

<u>Rule #4:</u> *A keyword AND search is used to search for data that relates two top-ics or concepts together. The data found will show the effect of the rela-tionship of these topics.*

An **AND** search is a limiting kind of search. It asks the computer to give data only when that data contains *all the* keywords linked by **AND**. Thus, you should expect that an **AND** search will give you fewer hits than if you had searched each keyword on its own. This is a difficult concept for many people to grasp. If you're having trouble with it, go back up to the **AND** search dia-gram above. Or consider the example above: you don't want every piece of data about homeless youth plus every piece of data about education. You want only the data that relates homeless youth to education. Thus the **AND** search has set limits for your search. It has narrowed down the data that you want to receive.

<u>Rule #5:</u> *AND searches will narrow or limit your topic. Thus you can expect that you will not get as many "hits" with an AND search as with an OR search.*

The NOT Command

I'm back to looking for information about cars, but I'm *not* interested in any car made in Europe (Please don't send me cards and letters asking why I have a problem with European cars—it's a long story). With this search, I want to tell the computer to give me everything about cars but no data about European cars. Here's how to do a **NOT** search:

(cars or automobiles) not Europe*

Notice what I've done. First, I remembered that "automobiles" is a synonym for "cars." Thus I included both, putting them in parentheses so as not to con-fuse the computer as to what I meant by my **NOT** command. Then I added the **NOT** and did a truncation on Europe (using an asterisk) so the computer could look for "Europe" and "European" with a single search. What I'm saying is that I want data about either cars or automobiles as long as it doesn't refer to European cars or automobiles.

Exceptions to the Above

Exceptions? Why are there always exceptions? Probably because every database likes to do its own thing. Here are some variations that you may find to the standard Boolean OR, AND, NOT searches:

❖ Some databases want you to put your linking words in capital letters—OR AND NOT (If in doubt, use capitals anyway.)

❖ In many databases, you can do an AND search simply by leaving a space between words. Instead of:

> **homeless youth and education**

you can type: **homeless youth education**

But note that some other databases will see homeless youth education *as a single phrase, thus requiring you to put the AND back in between "youth" and "education.*

❖ Some of the less sophisticated Internet search Engines use + and - signs. Thus

> +"homeless youth" +education = homeless youth and education

> +cars +automobiles -Europe = (cars and automobiles) not Europe

❖ In some databases, NOT has to be expressed as AND NOT.

❖ Some databases ask you to put quotation marks around words that need to appear together, e.g.:

> "apple trees"

Others call for parentheses: (apple trees).

❖ There are some databases now that actually search for synonyms of the term(s) you input so that they can bring up material you might not have found through a simple keyword search.

❖ Some databases provide a choice of buttons under the search box, like this:

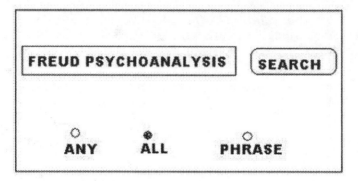

Complex Keyword Searches

Many databases now allow you to build your own search. They do this through a grid arrangement that allows you to specify *what type of words in what types of combinations you want to search*. Don't worry, it's not nearly as horrifying as it looks. Let's consider an example, remembering that the look and features of these search grid formats vary depending on what database you're searching.

Here's part of an "Advanced Search" screen from a database called "Academic Search Premier," produced by EBSCO Research Databases

Note that you can click your mouse button on the downward arrows on the right hand boxes to open options like **SU Subject** or **TI Title**. If you click on the type of search you want, it will appear in the search box.

Let's decipher the above search, which is:

Default Fields—Skinner
Subject—Behaviorism (Psychology)
Title word—Agoraphobia

I am asking for the keyword anywhere *Skinner* or the subject heading *Behaviorism* as long as either term is also associated with the article title word *agoraphobia* (the fear of going out into crowds). In other words, I want to know what either Skinner (a behaviorist) or the therapy of Behaviorism have to say about agoraphobia. In a standard Boolean search line, it would look like this:

Skinner and (SU)Behaviorism (Psychology) and (TI)Agoraphobia

Natural Language Searching

Natural language searching is a variation on the standard keyword search. It tries to imitate the way you would ask another person a question. Rather than inputting a few important words in a certain combination, it lets you simply ask a question, for example:

"What was the name of the Lone Ranger's Horse?"

Computers are not intelligent. They don't actually see a formulated question when they look at the sentence above. Rather, a natural language program picks up on keywords—"name," "Lone," "Ranger's" "Horse"—and formulates an AND search for you. A few databases and even some Internet search engines are playing around with natural language searches. For your part, you're probably better off learning to use Boolean terminology, which tend to be more precise.

Some Final Hints

❖ Before you begin a search, you need to think: "What is this topic about? What are the important words that define it?" That is, you need to *label* your topic with its favorite jargon.

❖ Consider whether or not you are connecting two or more concepts in unusual ways in dealing with your topic (e.g. Behaviorism and agoraphobia). If you are, a controlled vocabulary will probably not work as effectively as a keyword search.

❖ Discover the narrowest possible terminology to describe your topic. If you are dealing with *Martin Luther,* don't search for *Church History*. If you want information on *homelessness,* don't search for *social problems*. Be as specific as you can in determining exactly what you need. If your database search turns up any more than about 100 "hits," you probably need to find more specific terminology. I can't believe how many times I've seen students working through 500 or more hits, **one at a time!** Can there be anything more numbing to the mind, damaging to the eyes, and carpal tunneling to the wrists?

❖ If you are doing a keyword **AND** search, or a complex keyword search using a grid, remember that the more information you put on the screen, the fewer hits you will get.

❖ In most cases, believe it or not, controlled vocabularies will get you more and better results than will keyword searches. Keywords may be hot, but they are ultimately quick and dirty in their results. If you don't believe me, then why do most Internet keyword searches net thousands of results per search?

❖ Database searching is supposed to be <u>FUN</u>. If you're experiencing some other emotion, read this chapter again, cheer up, swallow your fear or boredom, and get out there searching.

For Further Study

Study Guide

1. What is a "database?" Name a few examples of familiar databases.
2. You can browse a telephone book easily. Why is a computer database more difficult to browse?
3. What are "controlled vocabularies", and what is the most familiar example?
4. How are controlled vocabularies created?
5. Why doesn't the actual title of the book matter a great deal when a cataloger attaches a controlled vocabulary term to it?
6. What are the advantages of controlled vocabularies?
7. In Library of Congress Subject Headings, what do the following abbreviations mean?
    UF BT RT NT
8. In keyword searching, what strong ability of computers is used?
9. What is a "truncation" or "wildcard?" Give an example along with the appropriate symbol.
10. Explain the "OR command" in Boolean searching and indicate in what types of searches it works best.
11. Explain the "AND command" in Boolean searching and indicate in what types of searches it works best.
12. Explain the "NOT command" in Boolean searching and indicate in what types of searches it works best.
13. Some databases will allow you to leave out the Boolean AND, and just input keywords with spaces between them. In other databases, if you do this the computer program will understand that you are constructing a
    _____.
14. What is "natural language searching?"
15. Do you really understand database searching? Since the principles of Chapter Two are so important to all modern research, go over the chapter again and again until you grasp the principles well.

Practice with Databases

1. Use Library of Congress Subject Headings to find the authorized subject heading for the following:
    a. LASH ships

    b.   Zen arts
    c.   Clothes hangers
    d.   Means used to prevent criminal activity
    e.   Canadian Religious Poetry
    f.   Books on being a catcher in baseball
    g.   Books on how to write for people who are newly literate
    h.   Pencilflowers
    i.   The philiosophy of Spiritualism
    j.   The Roman influences on law in the United States

2.   How would you formulate a keyword search to get results in a database on the following?

    a.   The causes of World War One.
    b.   Destruction of the museums in Iraq during the 2003 war.
    c.   The role of crime in the novel, *The Great Gatsby*
    d.   The problem of fear in patients with the psychological disorder paranoia.
    e.   Teen violence.
    f.   The movie, *Vanilla Sky* (as opposed to the painting, *Vanilla Sky*).
    g.   Kidney stones in Schnauzers.
    h.   Racial conflict in London.
    i.   Relationship between unemployment and homelessness in San Diego.
    j.   Stravinsky's musical composition, *The Rite of Spring*.

Suggested Key to Practice with Databases

1.   Library of Congress Subject Headings—Correct Headings

    a.   See: Barge-carrying ships
    b.   See: Arts, Zen
    c.   See: Coat hangers
    d.   See: Crime prevention [this one actually required you to think through some possibilities and test them—sorry].
    e.   See: Religious poetry, Canadian
    f.   See: Catching (Baseball) [made you think again, sorry.]
    g.   See: Writing for new literates [by now, thinking is seeming almost normal to you.]
    h.   See: Stylosanthes
    i.   See: Spiritualism (Philosophy)
    j.   See: Law United States Roman influences

2. Keyword Search Terms (My Suggestions)

    a. This is actually a tough one because you can call this war World War One, World War I, WWI, and even The Great War. Most of these descriptors are actually phrases, and it may be hard to combine them in a search in a database while maintaining their identity as phrases. You may have to search each descriptor in turn, e.g. World War One AND Cause* (notice the truncation), then World War I AND Cause*, and so on.

    b. Likely you can get by here with as little as Museum* AND Iraq AND War. Don't worry about the 2003, since the 1990 Iraq war did not raise the issue of museums, so the database will have no problem distinguishing the two wars.

    c. The name Gatsby is rare. In this case, you don't need to fill the search with terms. Simply try Gatsby AND Crime.

    d. You have a real problem with the term Paranoia, since it is widely used in contexts other than psychology. Thus, a search like Paranoia AND Fear could create a lot of irrelevant hits, among which will be a few that deal with the psychological disorder variety of paranoia. But don't think adding terminology like Psychological Disorder will help the situation. It won't, simply because keyword searches look for *words*. It's unlikely that the writers of an article on fear issues in the psychological disorder of paranoia will use the title, "Fear Issues in the Psychological Disorder of Paranoia." The title will much more likely be "Fear in Paranoia," or something similar. A solution? If the database uses controlled vocabularies, you might try a subject search on Paranoia as a psychological disorder and add the keyword Fear.

    e. Try (Teen* OR Adolescen* OR Youth) AND violence—Note the use of truncation and the choice of synonyms in an OR search.

    f. Try Vanilla Sky AND Movie, or even Vanilla Sky AND Cruise [because it starred Tom Cruise.]

    g. You could try Kidney AND Schnauzers. If that generates too many useless results, try Kidney Stones AND Schnauzers. With AND searches, always try to make it as simple a process as possible.

    h. Try Race AND London, but there is a potential that "race" may bring up material on racing. Perhaps Racial AND London would work more effectively. Avoid adding terminology like Problems, Issues, and so on, since title terminology of your data rarely uses such terms.

    i. Try Unemploy* AND Homeless* AND San Diego.

j.   For this one, continue the principle that short and simple is better than filling a search with terminology. Since this composition is distinctive, Rite of Spring should be enough. If it's not, add **AND Stravinsky**.

Assignment for a Research Project of Your Own

1.   State a research question on a topic of your choice. Have a good look at it and determine exactly what you want to search for
2.   Do a _title keyword_ search for books in a library catalog by:
     a.   Choosing important words related to your topic, and doing searches by these words either individually or in Boolean combinations. _Indicate the actual searches you tried, e.g. (Skinner or behaviorism) and Walden)_
     b.   Listing 8-10 books, **relevant** to your topic, which you identified through your keyword search. Keep as narrowly focused on your research question goal as possible.
3.   Do a _Library of Congress Subject Heading_ search for books in a library catalog by:
     a.   Choosing Library of Congress subject headings related to your topic and entering them in the Subject Heading search box/.
     b.   Listing 8-10 books, **relevant** to your topic, which you identified through your subject heading search. Keep as narrowly focused on your research question goal as possible.
4.   If you found less than 8-10 books for either part of this assignment, or if you struggled with locating the right materials, comment on why you think the difficulty occurred. Here, you need to identify any problems you see in your results or your methods.

3

Blowing Away the Information Fog
—Information hierarchies, library catalogs and bibliographies

Be honest. Are you into this yet? Do you really want to learn how to be a researcher? Anyone who does research needs to reckon with the fact that the process can be a struggle. For most people it's only slightly less painful than being flogged with barbed wire. A big part of the problem, I've found, is that many beginning researchers have no idea where they are, and if they finally arrive, they can't tell you where they've been.

Research, for many of us, is like driving through a fog. You know a concrete world exists all around you, but you can't feel it or see it because of all the data, ambiguous or undefined, that swirls around you. The signposts are obscured, and even if you find your destination, you have no idea how you got there. A lot of research is like that—trial and error based on confusion. No wonder it's so painful.

A better analogy for good research is the method a player uses in beating a video game. At each level, you adopt strategies intended to move you on to the next level. Once you've been playing for awhile, you find that you've developed a keen sense of where you are going and what it will take to get there. As each level is conquered, you move closer to that magic moment when you've beaten the whole game.

So how do you blow away the fog and start playing the game in earnest? Actually, some of the most important strategies are already part of your arsenal—Getting a working knowledge of your topic, developing a research question, putting together a preliminary outline, beginning to search the library catalog. So let's move on into new territory.

Finding your Way in an Information Hierarchy

If you want the fog really to be gone, you're going to have to learn some theory about the way information is structured. *Theory?* you say. *No way! This is supposed to be a practical book about getting research done efficiently and (hopefully) in a hurry. Theory will only get in the way.*

Before you give up that quickly, let's see what theory can do for you. Here's a question: Can you define the following word?

ROCK

"Sure," you say. "It's a hard object that comes out of the ground."

To which I answer, "How wrong you are! Don't you know that 'rock' is a verb? My definition, a symptom of my growing age, is that the only rock worth anything is the rock I do in my rocking chair.

"I'm not wrong," you retort. "You're wrong."

To which your friend standing next to us says with a smirk, "You're both wrong. It's music. Classic Rock is real music, and I'd rather be listening to it than wasting time listening to you argue about word meanings."

What's the problem here? Why can't we agree on a definition for one word with only four letters in it?

The reason is simple:

> Words by themselves don't really mean anything for certain. They only have a definite meaning when you put them in a context.

If I say, "I'm planning to take a whole evening to rock in my rocking chair," you know that my definition of 'rock' is something like 'a back and forth motion.' If, on the other hand, I say, "The rock that went through my window was two inches across," you know that 'rock' is now a noun meaning 'a hard substance taken from the earth.'

Words get their meaning from the sentences surrounding them. In turn, sentences become understandable within their paragraphs, and paragraphs make sense within the larger context of the complete document. The important word here is "context." Meaning is derived from context, and without context we have only confusion.

So what? How do meaning and context relate to research? Exactly like this:

> All data comes within a context. Without context the data cannot tell us what we need to know.

If you want to get technical, all data exists within one or more information hierarchies. Let me illustrate with the word "rock."

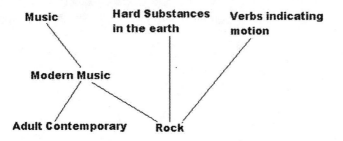

"Rock" is always a sub-class of something more comprehensive. For example, "rock" may be a sub-class of modern music, right alongside other sub-classes like "adult contemporary," "elevator music," and the compositions of John Cage. "Modern music" in turn is a sub-class of the larger category of "music" along with other sub-classes like "classical," "baroque," etc. What we end up with is a hierarchy. Each higher grouping is more general than the one below it.

But notice that "rock" is capable of having several different hierarchies attached to it, depending on the meaning we give to the word. It can also be a sub-class of "hard substances in the earth" or of "verbs indicating motion."

Let's now move into an area that better resembles a research topic. Take something like the Roman emperor Constantine. Depending on how you approach him, he can exist within a number of contexts (= hierarchies):

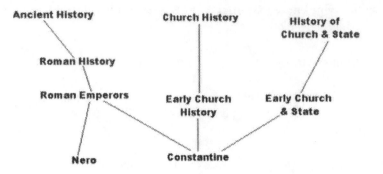

You can deal with him as a sub-class of "Roman emperors" alongside other sub-classes like Julius Caesar and Nero. "Roman emperors" in turn are a sub-class of "Roman history", which in turn is a sub-class of "Ancient History."

Alternatively, you can deal with him as an important figure within the larger subject of "Early Christian Church History," since he was the emperor who affirmed Christianity so that it could eventually become the official Roman religion.

Or you can discuss him within the higher class of "History of Church and State," since his marriage between empire and Christianity led to many issues related to the wisdom of creating such unions.

Each of these hierarchies leads to a different approach to the same topic.

All information is hierarchical. The rule is simply this:

> In research, you must always know where you are in the hierarchy.

What higher class does your topic belong to? Are there other hierarchies your topic could belong to? Are there sub-classes of your topic that could become factors to consider?

Take "homelessness." This topic might belong to a higher class of the "sociology of cities" (since most of the homeless seem to live in cities). "Sociology of cities" in turn is a sub-class of "sociology." But "homelessness" could exist within other hierarchies, e.g. "government policy toward the poor," or "issues of housing in modern society," or "current issues in social work." In turn, "homelessness" could have sub-classes such as "relationship between homelessness and rent control policy" or "services to those who choose to remain homeless" or "education of homeless children."

This is how we would diagram it:

The reason for all this discussion of hierarchies is simply this:

> If you know where you are, you can find your way to where you should be.

Let me show you how this could work with the topic of "homelessness:"

Once I have identified the issues related to the topic and developed a working knowledge, I choose to deal with the issue of providing an education to children in homeless families, particularly families which are in and out of temporary shelters set up for people without homes. Now I need to ask myself, "Who would be interested in working with such children?" Obviously the educational system wants to educate them, but it is doubtful that school boards themselves search out such children. Thus, this topic, while educational in nature, is likely not directly in the following hierarchy:

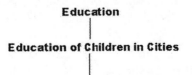

Rather, it will probably be social workers involved with such families who will work to make sure that these children are put into an educational setting. Thus the hierarchy we are looking for is something like this:

Social Work
|
Social Work with Families
|
Social Work with Children in Homeless Families
|
Educational Needs of Children in Homeless Families

Once I have identified the discipline within which the subject is best treated, I have some idea where to go. I may have to look for Social Work policy statements on the issue, books on the social needs of homeless children, perhaps even interviews with people involved in working with children in this situation.

Let's look at another topic. You are in an ethics class and you need to do a research paper on "abortion." It sounds simple on the surface (which should have been your first clue to run for the hills). But you quickly find yourself bogged down in tons of detail and zillions of issues. You could, I suppose, simply chronicle the history and major issues of the abortion debate, but your paper will be a superficial regurgitation of your sources, nothing more. You need a *focus*.

This is the time to begin brainstorming possible hierarchies within which abortion could be discussed, along with possible research questions you could ask (but remember to choose only one):

Philosophy: In relation to abortion, how do we define personhood? Is a fetus a person? If abortion is a matter of the relative value placed on completing a pregnancy as opposed to allowing women freedom with their own bodies, what values are being communicated?

Ethics: Can human beings ethically assert the right to continue or terminate a pregnancy? Is it true that advocating the right to abort a fetus is a "slippery slope" leading to euthanasia of the disabled and elderly?

Psychology: Is it true that an unwanted child can bring psychological harm to itself or its mother by being allowed to be born? Are the psychological after-effects of abortion harmful to a woman's future well-being?

Law: Does the allowing of partial term abortions fit properly with other laws of the land? How well do existing abortion laws protect the rights of all concerned? Can abortion laws protect the rights of prospective fathers when their wishes are opposed to the wishes of prospective mothers?

Religion: How do the Christian views of life relate to Muslim views with regard to abortion? How logical is the Evangelical Christian or Catholic argument against abortion?

Hierarchy is virtually everything when it comes to grappling seriously with a topic. You must ask yourself from the outset, **"What is this topic a part of?"** Once you can determine which hierarchy you want it to fit into, you can begin addressing it with focus.

Hierarchy can help in another way: If you can't find a book particularly on your topic, you may be able to find a book dealing with a higher level of the hierarchy. For example:

> If you can't find a book on Constantine, you might find a book on Roman Emperors or Roman History of his era or Early Church History.

> If you can't find a book on Abortion, you might find one on Medical Ethics

In a pinch, though it sounds goofy, you can do a spatial trick in a library that might help you a lot. Find the specific place in your library where your topic should be treated. If there aren't enough books to satisfy you, *move to the left.* Why? Because classification systems in libraries move to the right from the general to the specific. If you back up by moving to the left, you will move *up the hierarchy* to the more general discipline out of which your topic came. This doesn't always work, but it can be a helpful strategy when you're desperate.

Strategies to Clear the Fog in the Book Collection

Books tend to create fogs of misunderstanding, because they're blunt instruments. In order to write a book, you need a topic broad enough to be covered in a couple of hundred or more pages, but you need enough focus to avoid it becoming multi-volume or being superficial. Thus finding a book on your narrowed down topic that is driven by a research question may well be a challenge.

Generally, you need to assume that few books will be exactly on your topic. That is why strategies are needed.

Making the Catalog Work For You

Choices, choices—keyword or controlled vocabulary?

If your topic is somewhat standard, you will probably do best with a controlled vocabulary subject heading search. It's safer in that you know you will find most books that are available on the topic. The only problem is that the chances are you will only need a portion of the information found in each book. For example, if your research question is, "What's right and wrong with B.F. Skinner's utopian vision in his book *Walden Two*?" you might well find that there are few books available specifically on *Walden Two*, and you are going to have to do a controlled vocabulary subject search on **Skinner, B.F. (Burrhus Frederic), 1904**–and then study within books describing his thought to see what they say about *Walden Two*. Of course, you'll also need to look at *Walden Two* itself.

If your topic is not a standard one or if it combines a couple of subject disciples (such as the influence of *Walden Two* on the 1960's hippy movement), you may want to go for a keyword approach. Here are a few warnings, however:

❖ If you are working in a small library, keywords are less useful, since they tend to target specific and/or non-traditional approaches to topics. The library may not have enough diversity to meet your particular quirky need.

❖ Remember always that keyword searching, while it may narrow down your quest to exactly what you want, is a very inexact science. You have to have the right word(s) configured in the right way, and you are highly dependent on the actual terminology of titles in the collection.

❖ Be sure you don't use too many keywords at once. Start with one or two, and if that doesn't give you what you want, try one more. Rarely will you need more than three.

❖ Never forget that, in an AND search, every time you add a term you eliminate data from your results. This may be good if you have too many hits, but be careful to determine that the data you are eliminating is not crucial.

It's better to have more results and have to weed through them to find what you need than to have a smaller set of results that don't contain crucial data.

Above all in catalog searching, use lateral thinking. What we have covered in information hierarchies, above, should help you if you ask yourself one or more of the following questions:

➢ What hierarchy or hierarchies could this topic be a part of?

➢ If I can't find a book specifically on my topic, what topic is next above it in the hierarchy?

➢ If one approach is not working, what are other ways that I might look at the topic? (i.e. what other hierarchies could potentially contain the topic?)

Using Other People's Work Without Cheating—The Bibliography Search

Did you know that advanced scholars rarely do subject or keyword searches in catalogs? Before you assume that the problem is that advanced scholars are old and therefore have the same knowledge of the computer as a Neanderthal, let me assure you that this is not the case. Many advanced scholars know their way around computers pretty well. The reason they don't use catalogs very much is that they don't need to.

Imagine yourself as an advanced scholar. You've been working on your topic for years, maybe decades. You regularly read just about anything of importance that's published in your area of scholarship. You know who your key fellow scholars are. If you want to continue keeping up with your field, how do you do it? By picking up a colleague's latest book or periodical article and reading it. Not only that, but you search out what your colleague is reading by pouring over his/her bibliography and footnotes.

The reason why advanced scholars rarely do subject searches on their fields in library catalogs is that they are too busy reading the works and bibliographies of other scholars. This suggests another approach to searching for information on a topic—*making use of other people's bibliographies.* This is not theft or pla-giarism—it's research.

Here's a strategy that could net you a whole host of materials:

➤ Find a recent book on your topic. If there is no such thing in your library, find a recent reference book article with a bibliography, or a periodical article with footnotes (some periodical indexes are now providing a link to an article's footnotes along with the citation to the article, so you can do this strategy without even having the original article).

➤ Take note of the footnotes and/or bibliography and write down the citation for anything that looks relevant to your topic.

➤ Here's the potentially tricky part, so light up a few more brain cells: Actually *find* some of the items you jotted down from the above step. (These may be books or periodical articles or whatever). Open them and study *their* footnotes and/or bibliographies.

➤ Jot down any further items which interest you, locate them, and carry on the procedure until you wear yourself out.

Let's try an example:

You're working on the issue of spousal abuse, particularly the issue that women are often very hesitant to report the violence done to them by their spouses. The particular goal of your research is to discover principles that could be used in counseling such women to feel empowered to report abuse.

You discover, Aysan Sev'er, *Fleeing the House of Horrors: Women Who Have Left Abusive Partners.* Toronto: University of Toronto Press, 2002. It has an extensive bibliography, including:

L. Chalmers and P. Smith, "Wife Battering: Psychological, Social and Physical Isolation and Counterbalancing Strategies," in *Women: Isolation and Bonding: The Ecology of Gender,* ed. K. Storrie, pp. 15-38. Toronto: Methuen, 1987.

Kathleen J. Ferraro and J.M. Johnson. "How Women Experience Battering," *Social Problems* 30 (1983): 325-328.

David Finkelhor, "The Main Problem is Still Underreporting, Not Overreporting," in *Current Controversies on Family Violence,* ed. R.J. Gelles and D. R. Loseke, pp. 273-287. Newbery Park: Sage Publications, 1993.

Rosemary Gartner and Ross MacMillan, "The Effect of Victim-Offender Relationship on Reporting Crimes of Violence Against Women," *Canadian Journal of Criminology* 37, no. 3 (1995): 393-429.

Dee Dee Glass, *All My Fault: Why Women Don't Leave Abusive Men*. London: Virago Press, 1995.

And so on…

Notice what we have: Two of the titles are essays in books, which are notoriously hard to identify in library catalogs. Would you have found them other than locating them in someone else's bibliography? Two of them are journal articles, again challenging to find (see Chapter Four). You've identified, as well, a book that is clearly on target. There were more—the above is only a sample.

Now you could actually locate the items in the list above and see what their bibliographies have to offer. I did that for Gartner and for Finkelhor and identified even more articles and books that were relevant, though now they dated from the 1970s and 80s.

When you work with bibliographies, you can continue the process indefinitely, depending on how broad your library's resources are, how many items you need, and how exhausted you are beginning to feel. But eventually one of two things will happen:

❖ You will find that the bibliographies begin to refer to books and articles that are older and are thus either unavailable or irrelevant (depending on your subject). Notice that you'll routinely see a rough progression in your searches above from newer to older materials as you move down the hierarchy.

❖ You may begin to see a lot of repeat citations. When you do see repeats, you know that you have likely discovered the most important works on the topic.

Why go through this kind of exercise at all? A library catalog search should usually give you enough books, shouldn't it? This may well be true if you want just a few items on a topic. But if you want more, there are three reasons why a book bibliography search could be helpful:

➢ Bibliographies tend to reveal which works are considered to be the more important or "standard" ones.

➢ It is entirely possible that some works you spot in a bibliography will be under a subject heading or classification number that you wouldn't have thought of using.

➢ Bibliographies often contain treasures—works or parts of works you might not have discovered on your own.

Now that I've convinced you, hopefully, that this approach can help, you might be wondering why you should search the catalog at all. Why not simply steal your bibliographies from other people? There are two good reasons not to make bibliography searching your exclusive method:

First, no writer is obligated to cite all the good books on a topic. Thus you may miss some very relevant material.

Second, authors can only cite those works available to them when they were writing. For more recent materials, you still need to use the library catalog

You really need to use both methods. Depending on the topic, one may pay off more richly than the other, but both have their own contributions to make.

Using Subject Bibliographies

In some instances, careful people who love minute detail have produced whole volumes of bibliographies on specialized subject areas. If there is one for your subject, you may well have one of the best tools for finding more items on your topic. You can locate such a bibliography by looking up your subject area in the subject catalog of your library and adding a sub-heading—"bibliography." Many libraries group their bibliographies in one area for quick access.

Subject bibliographies come in a variety of forms. The most useful provide a survey of the topic and then annotate (comment on) each bibliography entry, arranging entries under appropriate subdivisions of the subject.

A related form of good bibliography is the "research guide," which is either an annotated bibliography subdivided by subtopics, or a series of "bibliographical essays" which describe the subject area by referring to and describing key works in the field. The bibliographical essay can be valuable to you because of the amount of description and evaluation it provides.

From this point, we leave the good and move into the bad and the ugly. Here we have the bibliography that is not subdivided or has no annotations. While it may be better than nothing, it can use up a lot of your valuable time while you try to find what you want. At least it will give you a splendid opportunity for growth and development (should you desire another one).

Take note, as well, of the fact that periodical articles often provide state-of-the-art subject bibliographies, citing the most current research. By the end of the next chapter, you will know how to locate such articles.

There is one drawback with most published subject bibliographies: They are dated. If a completed book manuscript takes six months to two years to be published, it is already somewhat out of date when it is released. By the time it has been sitting on the library shelf for five years, it's really becoming a fossil. Thus subject bibliographies are best used for picking up the standard works of the past.

In this chapter we have been looking primarily at ways to find book literature. We now move on to those challenging (and dreaded?) periodicals.

For Further Study

Study Guide

1. Why do words by themselves have no definite meaning? How do they get a meaning?
2. All data comes within a _____.
3. Explain an "information hierarchy." Choose two or three topics and illustrate how each fits into one or more hierarchies (a diagram works best for this).
4. In research you must know where you are ____ _____ _____.
5. Observe the diagram on homelessness. What do you notice from the fact that it can exist within a number of contexts or hierarchies? How does the hierarchy chosen determine how you are going to deal with the topic?

6. If you can't find a book or other information on a narrow topic, how can moving up the hierarchy help you?
7. What are the advantages and disadvantages of using bibliographies and footnotes from already published works to enhance your own research bibliographies?
8. What are some of the formats in which subject bibliographies can come? Briefly describe each.

Practice with Hierarchies

1. Create some hierarchical diagrams for the following: Microsoft, Iraq, Arnold Schwarzenegger, Anorexia. Indicate three possible higher contexts and three lower.
2. Go to Refdesk.com and locate the "Fast Facts" section. Use hierarchical searching to discover answers to the following:
   a. Distance from Chicago, Illinois to Baton Rouge, Louisiana
   b. In what state is Uyo, Nigeria? (Hint: Use Thesaurus of Geographic names, enter the data, then activate the hierarchy).
   c. Use the Ethnologue index (under "Langages") to identify in what Nigerian state the language "Daba" is spoken.
   d. Who said, "Laugh and the world laughs with you, Weep, and you weep alone"? (Hint: A quotation source might help).

Suggested Key to Practice with Hierarchies

1. Microsoft—Higher categories: computer software, competition laws, successful companies. Lower categories: Office 2003, recent court cases seeking to break up Microsoft, secrets of Microsoft's success as a company.
   Iraq—Higher categories: Archaeology, Arab Nations, History of War. Lower categories: Destruction of museums in Iraq in 2003, Iraq's relations with Iran, the Iraq war of 2003.
   Arnold Schwarzenegger—Higher categories: Body building, actors, politicians. Lower categories: Arnold's methods to stay in shape, Arnold as comic actor, the 2003 California recall election.
   Anorexia—Higher categories: Weight loss, psychological conditions, social problems. Lower categories: The effects of weight loss in those with anorexia, the role of a certain life factor in Anorexia, the role of "thin culture" in the increase in anorexia.

2. a. Distance from Chicago, Illinois to Baton Rouge, Louisiana—Go to Fast Facts > Almanacs and maps > How far is it? Then enter your information.
    b. Type Uyo in the "Find Name" box and Nigeria in the "Nation" box. When you get your results, click on the "Hierarchy" icon. Your result should be:

TGN Hierarchy Display

‹ *back to previous page*   <u>Vernacular Display</u> | **English Display**

VIEW CHECKED RECORD(S)   CLEAR ALL

Click icons (⬚) to view the hierarchy. Check boxes to view multiple records at once.

- ☐ ⬚ <u>Top of the TGN hierarchy</u> (hierarchy root)
- ☐ ⬚ .... <u>World</u> (facet (hierarchical))
- ☐ ⬚ .... <u>Africa</u> (continent)
- ☐ ⬚ .... <u>Nigeria</u> (nation)
- ☐   .... ➡ <u>Akwa-Ibom</u> (state)
- ☐   .... <u>Abak</u> (inhabited place)
- ☐   .... <u>Aro Chuku</u> (inhabited place)
- ☐   .... <u>Eket</u> (inhabited place)
- ☐   .... <u>Ikot Ekpene</u> (inhabited place)
- ☐   .... <u>Opobo</u> (inhabited place)
- ☐   .... <u>Opobo Town</u> (inhabited place)
- ☐   .... <u>Oron</u> (inhabited place)
- ☐   .... <u>Uyo</u> (inhabited place)

The answer is Akwa-Iborn State.

c. Use the map in Ethnologue to drill down to African countries, then choose "Nigeria" and scroll down to Daba. The state is Adamawa.
d. Ella Wheeler Wilcox (1855–?). In this case, the hierarchy is refdesk > Quotations > Bartlett's Familiar Quotations, then look it up (putting quotation marks around the quotation helps).

Assignment for a Research Project of your own

Find a recent book or an article in a recent reference source on a topic of your choice. List down 4-10 items from its bibliography (books and/or articles) that you think might be relevant to you. The relevance of these items for your research question is **very** important.

Actually locate 2 of these items in the library. Look at the bibliographies (or footnotes) within the two items you have found and list 4-6 items from *each* that you think might be relevant to you. Be sure to keep these items relevant to your research question. *Note: if you are unable to find books at a certain part in the process, try one more recent book or article and do the process again. If you still have trouble locating further titles, write down what items you tried to find and explain why you think you had a problem.*

Assess your degree of success in adding to your bibliography with this method (e.g. Did you find anything unexpected? Were some titles repeated?)

4

Making Your Way Through the Periodical Maze

Just when you thought that finding books was trouble enough, someone is sure to suggest to you that there's another whole world of research materials crying out for attention—*periodicals*. Periodicals? I'm referring to magazines, scholarly journals, annual publications, and so on.

Even thinking of using periodicals in a research project may produce in you a shudder of horror. You imagine sitting down in front of piles of journals, thumbing through each one in an anguished quest for something (anything!) on the "The Implications for Generation Y of Max Weber's Approach to the Sociology of Cities." Hours later, in bitterness of heart and soul, you will emerge, red-eyed, with one article that is only vaguely relevant.

Periodical searching used to be done that way when your grandfather was a wee lad in school. Now things are very different, due to the development of periodical indexes.

Before we get to indexes, let's clarify what makes periodicals different from books. The two have many similarities: Often they're printed in the same format. Both have title pages and footnotes, etc. Both sit on shelves. Why then do they deserve separate chapters in a research book? For one simple reason—you can't catalog a periodical like you catalog a book.

When a librarian gets a new book for the collection, the book is cataloged and put on the shelf. After that, there is nothing to do but sign it out and check it back in until it falls apart. The cataloger's job is done. But a journal title *keeps on arriving* every week or month or quarter or year. By definition, it is *periodical*. You can't catalog it once and for all like you can a book, because it keeps changing as more issues are added to the growing collection.

While it might be possible for a librarian to assign a subject heading to each article in each periodical as it arrives and then to create a database so that you could find articles on any given topic, it just wouldn't be practical. No librarian has the time to create a separate database of all the library's journal articles. Thus we have the periodical index.

What Periodical Indexes Are All About

Each year, a number of indexers sit down in front of piles of periodicals (often related to a specific subject discipline, such as psychology or history or religion) and enter data about each article into computer databases searchable by subject (or author or title or keyword, etc.). By doing a search, you can generate a list of articles from various periodicals that are relevant to the subject you are studying.

Before we go much farther, we need to distinguish two terms: *data* and *interface*.

Data = words. Data makes up the content of the record that identifies and describes a periodical article; the record is then fed into the computer, and it doesn't change.

The *Interface* is what you actually see on the computer screen when you search for the data in a periodical index. It includes the screen display, search methods, and so on. Interfaces change constantly. What this means is that the screen may look different the next time you use the index. The instructions on use may be different. Even the methods you need to use to search the index may be different. The data inside the database is the same, but the means you use to extract it may be brand new. To deal with a new interface, do the following:

➤ *Read the instructions on the screen.* Look, as well, for anything that says "search tips" or "how to use this index," etc.

➤ Go back over the material in Chapter 2 on database searching. Does your new interface permit controlled vocabulary subject searching (clues will be reference to "subject headings," a "thesaurus," or to a "browse" function)? If you are to search by keywords, what sorts of Boolean operators are in use in this database?

➢ Try a search on a broad basis first, perhaps inputting only one keyword. If you get more than about 100 "hits" (citations to individual articles), look for a means to refine or narrow your search by adding more words. But be careful, in doing so, not to eliminate good data—it's better to have more hits than to miss crucial articles because you narrowed with too much vigor.

Some Tips on Periodical Article Citations:

A periodical article citation is simply a description of a periodical article with sufficient information to help you find it. While the format of a citation may vary, this is the information usually provided:

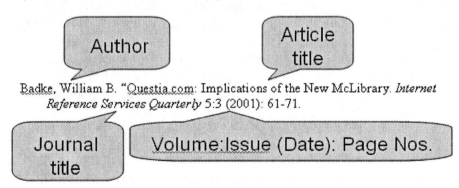

Badke, William B. "Questia.com: Implications of the New McLibrary. *Internet Reference Services Quarterly* 5:3 (2001): 61-71.

First we have data on the author and title of the article itself. Then we are told what journal it is in. We also have the volume number and issue number of the journal. Most journals are issued a new volume number for each year of publication, and there may be several issues released per year. In this case, 5:3 means volume 5, issue 3. Then you have a date and page numbers where the article may be found.

Full Text

We are now living in the next phase of computerized periodical indexes—Full text. Rather than simply listing citations to various journal articles, full text databases add the actual text of the article in electronic form—usually as HTML or PDF or both, the former looking like a re-typed document, and the latter looking like a photocopy of the original print version. You can even e-mail articles from your library to your home computer.

Before you begin believing that all periodical literature is now available to you in electronic form whenever you want it, take a reality check. The real world couldn't possibly be that accommodating. To tell the truth about full text:

- ❖ It's still pretty limited. Some journals are simply not available electronically. Others do have an electronic life, but your library may not have the right index that contains them.
- ❖ Back-runs are generally short, going back into the 1990s but rarely earlier.
- ❖ Format is a challenge—HTML loads faster in your computer but often doesn't contain graphics and loses the original page numbers, giving you only a starting page number and telling you the number of pages in the original. PDF has graphics and the original page numbers but loads slowly and generally creates a larger file than does HTML.

Many students are tempted to consider only journal articles that are available in full text, bypassing citations to articles the library may have in print or microform. That can be a mistake if the best article on a topic is only available in microfiche. It's wise to avoid taking the easy road just to finish your research early. (Why do I sense you're resisting what I'm telling you? Really. It's true—good, thorough research might demand using the occasional microfiche, but it's far more satisfying than simply getting the job done fast so you can go to a movie).

A First Adventure with a Real Live Computerized Periodical Index

If you want to learn to swim in the shark-infested waters of periodical literature searching, you have to arm yourself and just jump in. Let's look at a sample search using *EBSCO Academic Search Premier*, a user-friendly index with considerable full text content. By the time you read this, the interface may have changed, but the image below gives you a good idea of ways in which sophisticated indexes can do a good job of leading you to relevant journals.

Notice some of the features of this first screen:

❖ There is a box that allows you to enter information

❖ While this is a "basic search," with the "keyword" button depressed, you can also do an "advanced search" that allows you to build your investigation using Boolean terms.

❖ There is also a "subject" button, indicating that this index has a controlled vocabulary. In some databases, this will be called "Thesaurus." To help you identify the right subject heading, there will be a "browse" function that opens up when you click on "subject heading" or "thesaurus." Type in what you think the subject heading is, and you will be taken to the place in the list of subject headings where that term will be found. Generally, you can then click on the heading or put a check mark in a box to search that subject heading.

This is what a "browse" screen looks like:

Now let's have a look at the limiters and expanders:

Limiters and expanders simply narrow or broaden your search.

> You can limit to full text articles only, but never forget that the best article for your topic may not be in full text, so turning on this limiter could eliminate a valuable resource.
> You can limit to scholarly articles only (peer review refers to a process by which manuscripts submitted to a journal are checked out by experts in the field, who determine whether or not it is published—a great process for the journal, but nasty for the author of the manuscript, as my own scars will show).

> You can limit to a certain date range—though most indexes sort the found articles by most recent first.
> You can limit by specifying a certain journal.
> You can expand (broaden) your search by asking the search engine within the index also to search within the full text of articles that have full text. I usually turn this feature off—it tends to bring up a lot of irrelevant hits because the keywords I'm searching with appear somewhere in the text of the articles without those articles actually being about the topic I'm dealing with.
> You can search for related words ("s", "ed," and so on as endings).

Let's try out a search and see what we get. In the keyword box, type **wife abuse and police**. Limit by scholarly articles and turn off the expander that allows searching of the full text of articles.

1. USA. Police departments fail to arrest policemen for wife abuse. Women's International Network News, Winter99, Vol. 25 Issue 1, p40, 3/4p; *(AN 1521120)*
   HTML Full Text PDF Full Text **(171K)**

2. The dynamics of domestic abuse. (cover story) By: Marvin, Douglas R.. FBI Law Enforcement Bulletin, Jul97, Vol. 66 Issue 7, p13, 6p, 1bw; *(AN 9709240774)*
   HTML Full Text

3. Use of Police Services by Battered Women. By: Abel, Eileen Mazur; Suh, Edward K.. Social Work, Nov/Dec87, Vol. 32 Issue 6, p526, 3p, 6 charts; *(AN 5273025)*
   PDF Full Text **(290K) Times Cited (1)**

The result list includes three articles that look relevant. Let's look at the last one and be sure we understand it. The title of the article is "Use of Police Services by Battered Women." The authors are Eileen Abel and Edward Suh. The journal is entitled *Social Work*. The date is November/December 1987, it is volume 32, issue 6, and the article begins on page 526 and is 3 pages long. It has 6 charts in it.

In this case, the full text is available in PDF Full Text, which requires Adobe Reader to be loaded on your computer in order to read it (a free download off the Internet). PDF full text looks like a photocopy of the original print document. The other kind of full text—HTML—is a reformatted copy that loses the original page numbers but allows better searching of the text of the article.

Tips and Hints

➤ *Be prepared for frustration.* Periodical literature is not nearly as tidy as books are. Journals give you a never-ending supply of issues year after year after year, they can exist in a variety of formats (paper, microfilm, microfiche, computer files, Internet), and chances are the very article you need is nowhere to found in your metropolitan area.

Here's a psychological trick that might help you—*prepare yourself for frustration.* An illustration: If you are aware from long experience that you will face a traffic jam every day on the way to work, you are ready for it. It's only if a traffic jam happens unexpectedly in a spot you didn't expect that it frustrates you. In the same way, if you prepare yourself for periodical index frustration, you're less likely the mutter to yourself when it happens. Before you start using an index, say to yourself, "I know this periodical search is going to tax the last fragments of my patience, but it's good for me, it really is, it really, really is, and *I will succeed!*"

➤ *Resist the urge to fill the search screen with words.* Most keyword searches can be done with two words or, at the most, three. Remember this simple rule—the more you input into the search screen the more strain you're putting on your search. If it's an AND search, you are telling the computer that you want *only* those articles that have every word you've entered (which often results in zero hits). If it's an OR search, every article that has any one of your words will appear (resulting in thousands of hits sometimes). Get focused. Use as few words as you need to define your topic.

➤ *Look for controlled vocabularies and advanced searches.* These tools can help you to specify what you want, especially when keywords could be ambiguous. For example, if I searched EBSCO *Academic Search Premier* (a general subject index) for "paranoia," I would get a host of articles on all kinds of paranoia—political, social, suspicious spouses, people claiming to have been kidnapped by aliens, people suspicious of luncheon meats, and so on. If I could find a subject heading within Premier for the psychological disorder of paranoia (and I could), I would limit the field considerably. Now, if I tried an advanced search—SUBJECT Paranoia and KEYWORD Fear, I would find articles on the issue of fear among people with the psychological disorder of paranoia:

> *Think before you search.* Every new periodical index has a new interface, new search instructions, and so on. Even when you figure out how an index actually works, you need to think deeply about the terms you input. What will uniquely identify your topic in the minimum number of words? If your results show hit rates of 1,000 to 100,000 articles, you're aiming too broadly in your search, and you need to narrow down your terminology. If you are getting only one or two hits, you've probably gone too narrow by inputting too many search terms or asking for something so minute that there is only one scholar in the whole world who's remotely interested in the topic and she's on vacation.

> *Retrace your steps.* Be prepared to go back and figure out what you did wrong or how you could get better results. Look for buttons on the periodical index that allow you to "Refine Search" or "Search Again." Periodical index searching often demands experimentation to find just the right combination of terms that will nail down what you are looking for.

> *When in doubt, read the instructions.* Every periodical index worth its salt has instructions to guide you through the process of searching. When you've exhausted your own common sense, read the instructions. Different indexes have different capabilities and search techniques. You may find that the reason you get 354,000 hits one time and zero the next is that you are abusing the index by trying to make it do things it's not prepared even to contemplate.

> *Remain calm.* What's the most terrible thing that can happen if you blow a search? You might have to try again or (worst case scenario) one of your friends has watched you fail. Rarely will you have done any permanent harm to the index itself (unless you got violent, which is not recommended), so the only damage is to your time and your ego. If you find yourself hopelessly

lost, there is usually a reference librarian to help you out. Swallow your pride and ask for help. Having a bad day in front of an index isn't the end of the world. Above all, resist those evil thoughts that take up residence in your mind, such as, "I will never ever get this" or, "For people like me, ignorant would be a step up," "I must be a few pepperoni short of a pizza," or, "I want to break something." Cool your heart and try again.

➢ *Sometimes problems arise because you're using the wrong index.* An index of agriculture journals won't help you with a psychology project. A history index won't be much good if you're researching cockroaches. The right index for the right job is a rule not to be forgotten. If you can't find the right one, try a larger, broadly based, index.

➢ *Check out the possibilities of inter-library loan.* Not all academic libraries offer ILL, but if yours does, you may well be able to get the article you want by having it sent from another institution. There now, do you feel better?

Inside the New World of Periodical Indexes

The account of the history of periodical indexes used to be simple. It went something like this: "In the beginning, there were no periodical indexes. Then there were. You see those rows of volumes over there? Those are the indexes. Go use them."

Now the world is a much more complicated place. In what follows, I can only begin to acquaint you with the multitudes of changes occurring in modern periodical indexes, and what I say today could well be different tomorrow.

1. The Shift from Print to Digital

Most periodical indexes, even in the 1980's were accessible only in print format. Every year, a new volume of *History Index* or *Psychological Abstracts* or *Book Review Index* would arrive at your local academic library and be added to the volumes before it. If you wanted to search for a subject, you found the appropriate index (by its subject discipline) and then you started looking up your subject in volume after volume until you had compiled a list of relevant articles. It was great to have indexes available, but the tedium of searching, searching, searching really got to people. Another problem was that the subject you were searching often crossed the boundaries of subject disciplines (e.g.

"The effect of eagle migration on work schedules of conservation officers"), so you often had no idea what subject to look up.

Computers have solved many of these problems. With a computer, you should be able to input your search words *once* and search every year of the computer index all at the same time. You should also be able to combine keywords in new ways to narrow your search to exactly what you want.

And so, today, most periodical indexes you encounter are going to be digital. You're going to sit in front of a computer screen and input search data. The advantages are tremendous—better searches in a shorter period of time, the ability to save your results to a file or to print them, even the potential of getting access to the full text of articles in digital form.

There are some downers, though:

> There are dozens and dozens of interfaces out there. Every computerized periodical index seems to have a search screen that looks different from every other one, and even searches differently. While there are some attempts being made to standardize interfaces, you may find that you have to get to know a lot of different ways of searching as you move from index to index. Look closely at the search screen before you start. Use the "help" or "search tips" button to get as much information as you need. If your results are bad, don't assume that the index is useless or there is nothing available on your topic—try another search with new techniques.

> Computers tend to be something of a black hole. You send in a request, and the computer index tells you what it found (or didn't find). The index will rarely tell you what you did wrong. It won't give you three 6.5's and an 8 like Olympic judges do. At least with the old print versions of computers you could actually see the data that was in them. With computers, you need to be more savvy, and you also need to be prepared to try other options.

2. The Varieties of Indexes

At one time, the population of periodical indexes tended to be quite stable. You had your *Reader's Guide to Periodical Literature*, and then a whole host of subject discipline specific indexes:

Art Index   Historical Abstracts
Biography Index   Humanities Index
Biological Abstracts   Philosopher's Index
Social Sciences Index   Psychological Abstracts
Business Periodical Index   Religion Index One
Chemical Abstracts   Sociological Abstracts
Education Index

And so on. The only difference among them, other than subject, was that some offered abstracts (summaries of the articles) as well as citations to articles from various journals and others only had citations.

While many of the older indexes live on in computerized form, others have changed their names or combined with related indexes. There are some that are totally new and attempt to address new demands such as full text capability and delivery of articles to your home computer by e-mail. It's now virtually impossible to keep up with the types of indexes available or with their ever-changing interfaces. Staying in touch with research libraries and librarians seems to be the only way to remain up to date. Of course, for many people even the thought of keeping in touch with a librarian is repugnant, despite the fact that we're the nicest people in the world.

If you expect change in this area of research, you won't be disappointed. Despite the fact that it's hard for anyone to keep up, the abilities of these newer indexes are amazing and you can benefit greatly from them as long as you keep your wits about you.

3.   Full Text

Ah, the ever hoped-for, ever elusive dream of being able to access the full text of every article you need, right from your computer screen! It could be a reality right now but, alas, reality is never what we hope it will be.

Right now, you can go to an index, do a search and get a citation that includes not just the citation but the full text of the article. Click your mouse a few times and you can have the full text of the article either printed out or sent to your own e-mail address. The dream has been fulfilled, and you need never stalk through dark aisles of dusty bound journals again. Right?

Well, not exactly. While it is true that many indexes provide full text, there are still limitations on the titles and scope of the journals available in full text.

Why can't every article from every journal in the world be offered in digital form for minimal or no cost? To answer, let me give you a brief lecture in economics. Our world turns on our ability to manufacture things and sell them to other people. If we all worked really hard to produce things and then gave away what we produced, the world would stop spinning on its axis and life as we know it would disappear. Economics makes the world go around. Thus journal publishers, before they make their material available to vendors of full text indexes, demand to be paid and paid handsomely. Guess who ultimately bears the cost of each fee paid to each journal publisher—the library that subscribes to the index

We are now living in an era of serious transition for scholarly journals. Most of them have started to provide electronic versions via the Internet to people who subscribe to the print versions. The next step, over the coming ten to fifteen years will be the abandonment of paper subscriptions in favor of electronic full text subscriptions only. The smartest journal publishers are making deals with companies like EBSCO or ProQuest or InfoTrac or JStor to provide electronic access now. Alternatively, they can create their own electronic full text, charge libraries a full subscription price, and EBSCO or some other vendor can include them as a link within one of its databases. Some companies like Sage and Oxford, who have extensive journal holdings, are selling packages of electronic subscriptions to libraries. Any way you look at it, the print scholarly journal will soon be pretty much dead.

So much change, so little certainty. How did life get like this? To answer that question would force me to delve into philosophy and the history of culture, something I don't feel like pursuing right now. Why don't you do the research yourself and let me know?

4. Internet Indexes

"There's no need to bother with libraries anymore. Everything's on the Internet anyway. What's the point of going to a library or using a library web page from home to use a periodical index when there are tons of good periodical indexes on the Internet? It's too much bother anyway putting in my password just to get articles."

Bold opinions indeed, except that most of what you just said is based on some kind of urban myth, like crocodiles in the sewers of New York. There are relatively few periodical indexes available for free, without password protection, on the Internet. In fact, the only really big periodical index available at no charge on the Net is Ingenta (**http://www.ingenta.com**).

Other than Ingenta, periodical indexes on the Internet are few and limited in their ability to locate the articles you need. The indexes you use through your library may come to you via the Internet, but they are password-protected for a reason—your library has paid big money for subscriptions to them because they offer true quality.

Final Pep Talk

Don't be afraid of periodicals and periodical indexes. They want to be your friends. Scholarly articles in journals and magazines will provide you with a wealth of current and specific information that you dare not ignore. Just heed the following pieces of advice, and you will survive the periodical maze:

➤ Stay calm
➤ Stay focused
➤ Read the directions
➤ Plan your searches well
➤ Ask for help when you need it

For Further Study

Study Guide

1. How are periodical indexes created, and what are they intended to do?
2. Explain the difference between "data" and "interface."
3. Identify each part of the following periodical citation:

   William Badke, "International Students: Information Literacy or Academic Literacy?" *Academic Exchange Quarterly* 6, no. 4 (Winter 2002): 60-65.

4. In periodical index searching you should be prepared for _____. How does such preparation help you?
5. Why should you resist the urge to fill the search screen with words?
6. What are the advantages of thinking before you search?
7. More and more periodicals are being offered in "full text" format. What are some of the advantages and difficulties with accessing full text?

Practice with Periodical Indexes

Go to **http://www.ingenta.com/**and find their "step-by-step guide to searching." Follow these instructions and try a few of the searches they suggest, plus a few of your own.

If you have access to other periodical indexes through an academic library, spend time trying them out as well, consulting search instructions and using the various functions allowed by the index.

Assignment for a Project of Your Own

1. Choose a topic of interest to you.
2. Choose two periodical indexes. If you do not have access to university databases like those produced by EBSCO, ProQuest, and so on, choose from Internet-based indexes: **www.ingenta.com, http://www.findarticles.com/,** or **http://magportal.com/.**
3. After having a good look at their interfaces, do a periodical literature search with each.
4. Indicate what subject terms or keywords you used in your searches.
5. List 6 articles from each index that are relevant to your topic—author, article title, title of periodical, volume number, date, page numbers.

Note: Be sure the indexes you use are relevant to your topic. Not all indexes are relevant to any one topic.

5

Internet Research

The early 1990s saw the beginning of an information revolution as dramatic as the invention of the printing press in 1440 (though, typical of our narrow Western mindset, we usually ignore the fact that the Chinese had a printing press 400 years earlier). The printing press made it possible to replace the normal copying of documents by hand with a process that produced multiple copies at the same time. All of a sudden, the availability of written information increased dramatically.

The Internet in the 1990s created the same kind of revolution, but on a larger scale. An information delivery system primarily concerned with paper and print (libraries, bookstores, hard copy periodical subscriptions and so on) became an electronic universe available to anyone with a computer and a service provider. Today, the average student gets over two-thirds of his/her information from the Net.

Please supply your own answer to the following question: **The Internet is a world where:** _____

Stumped? Let me supply some possibilities:

The Internet is a world where:

> ➤ you can find information on virtually any topic
> ➤ almost everyone is trying to sell you something
> ➤ you can surf until your eyes fall out

> ➢ anything that's worth anything costs *money* to retrieve (or else you're told that access is "**forbidden!**")
> ➢ you can meet new friends
> ➢ you can't trust anyone or any piece of information
> ➢ you can get your questions answered
> ➢ you can waste a lot of time

Maybe your response should be "all of the above." The Internet is wonderful and frustrating, helpful and dangerous, beneficial and a waste of time. If keyword searching is the Wild West, the Internet is Dodge City. Why bother with it then? Because it is becoming the common denominator of our daily lives. What do I mean? All of us know that most transactions today are becoming digital—we use bank machines and online banking, we use computer library catalogs, and many of us are shopping from home over the electronic highway. As this phenomenon of doing things electronically grows (and it will), the only common medium that can meet its needs is the Internet. The Net will be the basis, the common denominator, for the things we need to get done.

Thus, love it or hate it, we'd better try to understand it.

> *Disclaimer:* In the pages that follow, several Internet addresses will be given. Addresses change rapidly on the Net, so I make no guarantee that you will find what you're seeking by inputting the addresses given. Sorry, but that's life, raw and nasty, though still interesting nevertheless. Check the update page for this book: **http://www.acts.twu.ca/lbr/updates.htm.**

A Brief Introduction to the Net

The Internet has been around for a quite awhile, but most people didn't know it until the early 90s.

Back in the late 1960's, the US military developed a worldwide computer network in order to remain in communication with everybody involved in the space program and defense research. This network (really a network of networks) eventually came into the hands of non-military people—scientists, computer buffs, and so on. It lacked a common communication language that was easy to use, so only specialists could profit from it. In the 1990's, a common communication language and a common communication protocol were established so that anyone who had access to this network could move around it with ease.

Let's consider some terminology:

Browser—a program that gives you access to the Internet and its searching tools as well as allowing you to manipulate and download data. Two common examples are *Internet Explorer* and *Netscape*. You'll find a browser as a button on your computer screen if you have Internet access. Double click on the button and your browser opens.

Home Page—The first screen you come to when you open your browser. It is also the front door or first room in any Internet site. From there you can click your mouse button on various things to be given further information.

Here's a part of a screen for the browser called Internet Explorer, including a home page. By the time you read this, the interface may have changed, but the basic functions will be the same:

There is a box in which you can insert an address, and the "forward" and "back" buttons to navigate around Internet sites you've already viewed. This is the "home page" for the electronic version of a portion of this book. I've also added a search engine toolbar from Google.

URL—Uniform Resource Locator. A specific "address" for a database or information site available through the Internet. It's analogous to a telephone number

that helps to link your phone with someone else's phone, except that, for an URL, you are linking computers. The typical URL begins with **http://**then has a distinctive alpha-numeric description in which there are no spaces. Thus, you can find the ERIC database if you go to the URL:
http:www.eric.ed.gov

How do you ask your computer to take you to a specific URL? Easy. There is an address box on your browser. Simply input the new URL you want to go to and click on the appropriate button or press "enter."

Search—Every browser (Internet searching program) has a "search" function. When you click on that function, you will be taken to a "search engine" or perhaps a whole menu of "search engines."

Search Engine—The Internet is a network of thousands and thousands of computers linked, essentially, through telephone lines or other cable systems. Each database held by one of these computers has an "address". But suppose that you don't know any addresses. You just want information on a topic. In that case a "search engine" is what you need. The average search engine asks you to input one or more keywords. When you click on the appropriate button, a search begins through thousands of networked computer databases (actually through the search engine's own indexed snapshot of the Internet), looking for the data called for by your keyword(s). You are then presented with a list of relevant database sites, with some summary information for each. You can click on each site in turn, and that site will be brought to you. Thus a search engine is like a servant sent from house to house to ask for something specific that you need.

More on search engines shortly.

World Wide Web—Often described as WWW. It is an organization system for sites on Internet, allowing a user with a search engine to find information from many databases using a common language (HTML) and a common method of communication (HTTP).

HTML—The common language of the World Wide Web. It stands for *HyperText Markup Language*. This is the common language by which data in the World Wide Web is written.

HTTP—*HyperText Transfer Protocol,* a formatting method to determine content and means of transfer of information on the Net. If we were to use the phone system as an analogy, http would be like the system that phone companies worldwide have agreed upon to make sure a phone in Nigeria can communicate with a phone in England. Http is the protocol that is used within the World Wide Web to allow communication among websites. Most Internet URLs begin with "http."

Document—On the Net, a document is any collection of information that you locate in your searching (home page plus related pages on one internet site).

Link—One of the neat features of the World Wide Web is that it allows you to move from one document to another by way of a *hyperlink* or just plain "link." A link in a document is a word or phrase with colored letters, generally underlined. When you point your mouse at a link, the mouse arrow becomes a pointing finger. When you click on the link, you will be taken to another document. Thus you can move from document to document without typing in a lot of addresses. This is often called "surfing the net" or "riding the information highway."

Bookmark—Your browser has a bookmark or "favorites" function that allows you to record the addresses of sites on the Internet that you want to return to. When you want to return, you can click your mouse on that bookmark, and you will be taken to that site without needing to type an address.

How can a person find out more about the Internet?

There are zillions of books in bookstores and libraries on every aspect of the Internet. As well, there are magazines solely devoted to the Net.

Try the following sites on the Internet for some good information on using it for research purposes:

http://www.learnthenet.com/english/index.html

(This one, called *Learn the Net*, is very informative and user friendly. It also has a lot of links to other information about the Net).

http://www.lib.berkeley.edu/TeachingLib/Guides/Internet/FindInfo.html

(Tutorial with links—University of California, Berkeley)

Searching the Internet

Searching by Search Engine, Using Keywords

In the most common Internet research situation, you want information on a topic, but you don't have a specific address. This is where a search engine can help you by taking the keyword(s) you input and searching the Internet for data that is relevant.

As you will soon discover, each search engine does the job a bit differently and with different results. Some search engines are better for certain searches than for others.

Some search engines *rate* the data they are giving you. That is, they assign probability percentages to tell you how likely it is that the search engine gave you what you asked for. Others do not rate the data.

Typically, you will get thousands of hits for any keyword search. Thus the search engines that *rate* your data and don't give you more than you asked for are better for most searches.

How do you input the keywords?

That depends. Each search engine has its own set of search paradigms. Most search engines have a "tips" or "help" or "about" link you can click on to be guided on the best ways to input keywords for that search engine.

❖ In most cases, the better search engines automatically create an AND. Commonly you can leave it out, but you have to specify OR, and NOT is often done with a dash in front of the NOT word (-trees). If you want to include in your search a word that is not normally searched (e.g. "the" or "of"), you will need to put a plus sign in front of the word, with no spaces: +the.

❖ A number of search engines allow you to group words that normally belong together. To do this, use quotation marks:'

    "accountability groups"

If you don't use the quotation marks, the search engine will also locate any articles that use the two words even though they are not related, as in:

"The president is calling for more *accountability.* This has been rejected by several *groups* of protestors who insist that…"

Always check the search tips for a search engine and make sure you know what you're dealing with. Some of them want you to input names in certain ways. Others want you to use capitals for proper names and titles. Most will allow you to refine your search if you find you're not getting what you want or you have too many hits.

A Basic Introduction to the best Search Engines

Truth to tell (and I usually try to do so, because I'm not a convincing liar), you could likely get by with Google (www.google.com) and never use another search engine. But it can be useful to attempt a search on another search engine once you've googled, just in case you missed something. Each search engine creates its own index of the Internet, so that, while Google is the biggest, it may not have indexed sites that are found in another search engine's index.

The best search engines are: Google, Vivisimo, Teoma, and AllTheWeb. By the time you read this, a new search engine (like up and coming Walhello) may have risen to the ranks of this really good ones, and the features of the four best may have changed. But I dare to introduce them to you anyway, brave fool that I am. Here goes:

    Google (http://www.google.com/)

Google has the biggest index of the Net and consistently does the best job of locating what you're searching for. Here are some key features:

- As you input keywords to use as search tools, Google automatically forms them into an AND search and seeks to bring you websites that contain those words in close proximity to one another.
- Google uses a technique called PageRank that prioritizes your results by giving you first those sites that are most often found as links on other websites. This "popularity" measure really seems to work in most searches so that the most relevant sites appear in the first 20 or so results.
- Google offers simple techniques to create Boolean searches:
  —AND is automatic
  —You can create an OR by inputting OR in capital letters. Google cannot, however, group searches with () as in Freud AND (ego OR id). You are best to do separate searches in such situations.
  —Phrases can be searched by putting quotation marks around them, e.g. "apple trees." This is true of all the best search engines.
  —You can't truncate search words, e.g. educat* for education, educator, etc.
- Ever have the problem of discovering a site with a search engine only to get a "Not found" message, possibly indicating that the site has been closed or has moved? If that happens in Google, you can click on the "Cached" link in the Google results list and get Google's snapshot of the website as it was when Google last indexed it.
- Google offers a toolbar that you can download and install at the top of your browser. With it, you always have a Google box to do a search any time your browser is open. But there's more: The search terms you use appear on the toolbar so you can click on one of them and be taken to all the places in a document where that word appears. There is a separate search button on the toolbar that lets you do a search only within a website you currently have open. The toolbar can even limit the number of "pop-ups" you experience (those annoying ads that pop up without you asking for them). Only the rare computer I ever use escapes without me adding a Google toolbar to it.
- Google has a killer "Advanced Search" feature that helps you do all sorts of things:

  ✓ The "Find Results" options let you build complex Boolean searches.
  ✓ You can specify the languages of the websites you want returned.
  ✓ You can ask for return of results only in specified formats (PDF, MS Word, PowerPoint, etc.), all of which are indexed in Google, unlike some search engines.
  ✓ You can select only the most recent websites.

✓   You can specify where you want your search terms to appear in docu-
      ments you retrieve.
✓   You can ask for only those sites belonging to a certain domain (regis-
      tered Internet name).
✓   You can even locate the websites that have links to a specified site.

All in all, Google is a winner. Newer features include Google Catalogs
(enabling you to locate manufacturers' catalogs on the Net), Froogle (to locate
products for sale), and links for specific searches within US Government or
University sites (on the Advanced Search page).

Vivisimo (http://vivisimo.com/)

Vivisimo is what we in the info biz call a "metasearch engine." It enlists the aid
of other search engines, using their search powers and indexing of the Net as a
means to gather as many relevant sites as possible. While the process is complex, we can think of it as if Vivisimo hired a bunch of professional searchers
(other search engines) and put them to work for a common purpose.

Vivisimo has a pretty good search function (though Google still indexes more
sites and consistently brings you more of the most relevant sites first), but
Vivisimo offers something that might make you smile in the midst of a tough
search with too many results—Document clustering through what it calls its
Clustering Engine.

This is what happens when you do a search: A limited number of sites are
retrieved—you set the limit yourself—and these are clustered according to
common keywords found in each group of sites. What this does is to organize
your results into clusters. For example, if I were to search on my name—
"William Badke"—they might be clustered like this:

"William Badke" (123)
Your Way Through The Information Fog (31)
Books (23)
Students (24)
Literacy, University (13)
Trinity, Associate (11)
www.acts.twu.ca (13)
Library Research (8)
Reference, Research Strategies (5)

Research Resources (3)
Research Guide (6)

Each of these would be a clickable link, to lead you to the web sites in that category. Information overload is conquered forever (or maybe not). Just recognize that nothing's perfect, so you can expect that there will still be problems. That's life, so you just have to get used to it.

Vivisimo offers some pretty good features:

- You can use common Boolean operators, including several variations:

   AND, +, and, or nothing do an AND search (thus the default for this engine is AND).

   " "around two or more words gives you an exact phrase search.

   OR, or do an OR search

   AND NOT, NOT do a NOT search.

- In Advanced Search, you can specify how many results you want returned, choose the search engines you want to engage, specify the language of results you want returned and customize your display.

   Teoma (http://www.teoma.com/)

"Teoma" means "expert" in Gaelic. Rather than adopting Google's principle of giving the highest rank to results that have a lot of links to them from other websites, Teoma uses "Subject-Specific Popularity." From their website, "Subject-Specific Popularity ranks a site based on the number of same-subject pages that reference it, not just general popularity." (**http://sp.teoma.com/ docs/teoma/about/searchwithauthority.html**).

Teoma uses a default AND (so + is not needed except if you want to include words that are normally not searched, such as +the). For NOT, use—.

Like Google and Vivisimo, Teoma has an Advanced Search function that allows you to build and limit your search.

Like Vivisimo, Teoma has a clustering system located at the end of the results it captures, though the system is not quite as sophisticated as Vivisimo.

Like Google, it has a downloadable toolbar for your browser, though the toolbar lacks the advanced features offered by Google.

AlltheWeb (http://www.alltheweb.com)

AlltheWeb boasts an index of over 3 billion websites. While its ranking system does not appear to work as well as Google to bring you the most relevant sites first, it does have a very sophisticated and complex Advanced Search function that allows you, among other things, to create a Boolean search (AND, OR, AND NOT); specify language, domains and media types to include or exclude; predetermine file formats for results; set dates, and even pre-set the maximum or minimum size of websites found. AlltheWeb also lets you search specifically for news, pictures, video, audio and FTP files.

Now, if we could only get all the best search engines to amalgamate and create one engine with all the best features of each of its parts…But then we'd have to start importing green cheese from the moon and having Christmas all year round. Until that happens, use Google first, but know when to move to one of the others.

Searching by Subject Tree

All information exists within hierarchies. For example, cell phones are a subclass of telephones which are a subclass of electronic communication devices, of which there are many others:

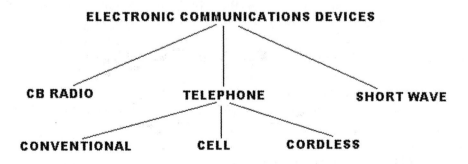

Do you see how such hierarchies can form a tree-like structure? There are certain sites on the Internet where you can search down various hierarchies or subject trees from more general categories to specific ones.

For example, Google, while majoring on keyword searches, also has a Directory tab that leads you to a list of categories like Art, Business, News, Science, and so on. Click on any one, and you can follow a hierarchy down to more specific information.

A growing area of significant development on the Internet is the "portal," a site that serves as an introduction to important Internet sites on a subject area (or even many subject areas). Typically, its main feature is a collection of links to sites that have been checked out for quality. What you end up with is a hierarchical way of searching the Net without a search engine. Its advantage is that someone has evaluated the sites, so you have a better chance of finding material that you can actually use (though your own critical thinking skills still need to be engaged—sorry, I'm sure you immediately assumed that using a portal meant you wouldn't have to do much thinking).

Some portals are organized by subject. Here are a few examples:

- Psych Wurld: MegaPsych Bookmarks (**http://www.tulsa.oklahoma.net/ ~jnichols/bookmarks.html**) is a psychology portal to websites categorized by type. Locate a category like Ethical Issues in Psychology, and you will be led to a page that subcategorizes web links under headings like Ethical Treatment of Humans, Ethical Treatment of Animals. Thus the whole thing is hierarchical and leads you ultimately to the website designer's collection of best links to a particular subcategory.

- European History (**http://www.lib.washington.edu/subject/History/tm/ europe.html**)

- Biology Online—Information in the Life Sciences (**http://biology-online.org/**)

- Wabash Center Guide to Internet Resources for Teaching and Learning in Theology and Religion (**http://www.wabashcenter.wabash.edu/Internet/ front.htm**)

and so on. But how do you locate such sites in the first place? Here's where a more general portal can help. A general portal is usually much larger, and often serves, at least in part, as a portal to lead you to more specific subject portals. For example:

About.com: **http://www.about.com/**, offers Internet guides to almost any subject you could imagine.

Infomine: Scholarly Internet Academic Collections: **http://infomine.ucr.edu/**, boasts over 100,000 academically valuable sites, organized by broad subject categories or searchable by its internal search engine.

Multimedia Educational Resource for Learning and Online Teaching: **http://www.merlot.org/**. This is a project of several universities and academic organizations to organize and peer review websites valuable for higher education. You can search it directly or hierarchically by subject categories

Academic Info: **http://www.academicinfo.net/**, is a educational subject directory to programs of study and test preparation sites. It includes a section of subject gateways to most disciplines

Librarians' Index to the Internet: **http://lii.org/**, searchable directly or by hierarchy.

Trinity Western University's guide to Internet sites by academic disciplines: **http://www.twu.ca/library/wwwsites.html.**

The Hidden Internet

You may have heard of the so-called "Hidden Internet" or "Invisible Web" or "Deep Web," that portion of the Net that only a few can see. Before you start thinking in terms of nasty conspiracies, recognize that there may be legitimate reasons for certain Web information not to be easily found.

What do we mean by "Hidden?"

A simple definition would be: "Any site not easily found by a search engine." Considering the fact that all search engines must first "discover" a site before they can index it, there is always a strong possibility that some sites will remain hidden. Beyond this are sites that search engines did find but that have deeper portions accessible only through a password.

What's the nature of Hidden Websites?

The Hidden Internet includes the following:

- ❖ Sites that are password protected—corporate intranets, subscription databases, banking information, e-mail accounts, and so on. These are protected either to maintain security or restrict access to patrons who have paid.

- ❖ Information within non-restricted databases such as library catalogs. A search engine may find a certain database, but it will not find individual records within that database, because the software of the database itself cannot be run by a search engine, only by you. So you might find the catalog of a university library with Google, but Google can't search that catalog automatically to find a record for a certain book. You have to search it yourself. In that sense it's both hidden but accessible.

- ❖ New or obscure sites not yet indexed by a search engine, or not indexed by the search engine you are using.

How do I find information on the Hidden Internet?

That depends:

- ❖ If it is a password-protected site, you need to be authorized or you'll need to pay to get access. Don't hack, please!

- ❖ Many searchable databases can be located either by search engine or by hierarchical searches on the Net (see the above section).

- ❖ Gary Price has put up a site called *direct search* (http://www.freepint.com/ gary/direct.htm) to guide you to sites that open doors to the Hidden Internet. Another useful guide is ProFusion (http://www.profusion.com)

The Hidden Internet lives, but there's no conspiracy. Really!

Evaluating Information from the Internet

Let's be realistic for a moment (aren't we always?) and ask the question: *Why would people with data want to put it on the Internet?* The answers are varied:

➢ They want to sell you something, and their web page is simply advertising or a doorway to a credit card purchase.

➢ They have something they want to say, and this a cheap and easy way to do it. Here you can have anything from *"Hi, I'm Tim, and here are some pictures of my car,"* to *"I was abducted by Martians, and I want to warn the world before they destroy us all."*

➢ A government or public agency that would normally not charge for its information wants to make it available. Here you can find everything from the ERIC index to telephone and directory information, census data, and so on.

➢ An educational body that sees providing information as part of their mandate. Here you may get journal articles, electronic editions of out of print books, guides to this and that, occasionally even electronic dictionaries or encyclopedias.

➢ Sincere scholars and other individuals who have valuable information to share and want to make that information freely available for the edification of everyone.

But take careful note of one foundational rule of life: **Few people, except those related to the last reason above, provide information for free on the Net unless they can't find anyone to pay for it or they have the financial resources to give it away freely.**

What does that mean for you, the anxious Internet searcher? It means several things:

♦ A lot of what you hoped might be on the Net is not there or you have to pay for it—the full texts of journal articles, the full texts of recent books, a vast array of reference tools, etc.

♦ Most keyword searches through search engines also bring you a ton of "garbage" that you have to weed through to find a few gems.

♦ It is much harder to evaluate the quality of the material you find on the Net.

Let's consider this latter point a bit more closely. In normal publishing, there are gatekeepers to make sure that material that is inferior doesn't get published (at least we hope there are gatekeepers—sometimes I wonder). On the Internet, anybody who wants to say anything has the chance to say it. Unless it is criminally obscene or violently racist, no one challenges it. Thus people can tell lies on the Net, and they probably won't suffer any nasty consequences (at least not in this life).

So what happens when you download a document that has no author listed but seems to be reliable information about B.F. Skinner's behaviorism? How do you determine whether it's good or bad information? Here are some clues:

- Look for the name of an author and/or organization responsible for the information. One way to do this is to recognize that Internet URLs are hierarchical and that the slashes in an address (/) define lower levels of the hierarchy. For example, the website advertising my book, *Beyond the Answer Sheet: Academic Success for International Students* (an example showing my penchant for blatant self promotion) has the URL **http://www.acts.twu.ca/lbr/answer_sheet.htm**. If I chop off the portion/ lbr/answer_sheet.htm, I have left **http://www.acts.twu.ca**, which is the educational institution that has allowed me access to their website (a foolish move on their part, but at least it gives me the appearance of being a genuine scholar). Chopping back on a URL will often lead you to the source behind the document you're interested in, though sometimes it just reveals the name of a person's Internet service provider, which, if it's some generic vendor of web space, will give you no help at all.

- Look for signs of scholarship—good language level, analytical thinking, bibliography and/or footnotes, logical organization.

- Look for signs of a **lack** of scholarship—lots of opinion without the support of evidence, indications of paranoia (as in *somebody's out to get us,* or *we're victims of a conspiracy*), poor spelling and grammar, lack of reference to other sources, poor organization. Ask yourself—does this person have a vested interest in promoting a viewpoint or is he/she simply sharing information?'

- Ultimately, you may have to evaluate the information itself. Does it make sense? Does it ring true? Is there sufficient backing for viewpoints presented? Have you or your professor ever heard of the people involved? Remember that Internet data may lack all the proper signposts of good scholarly work and yet still be valuable. On the other hand, it may have footnotes and a bibliography but be a racist rant. For proper evaluation, the buck stops with you actually reading the material and making sense of it.

- If you want to learn how to evaluate Internet resources, take The Internet Detective, a free website tutorial with quizzes and everything (**http://www.sosig.ac.uk/desire/internet-detective.html**). One thing to watch for—many pages in the tutorial appear to end at the navigation arrows but there is much more material if you scroll down farther.

Some Internet Addresses Valuable for Research Purposes

In presenting the following addresses, I must warn you again that addresses, like phone numbers, go out of date fairly quickly. On the Net, something you found today might not be there tomorrow. So some of these addresses may not work. If you have a problem, try searching for the title of the source, using a search engine.

❖ Reference Sources

The Internet Public Library—Ready Reference: **http://www.ipl.org/ref/RR/**

Internet Public Library index of 20,000+ books available full text on the Net: **http://www.ipl.org/reading/books/**

Refdesk, an amazingly detailed site that bills itself as "The single best source for facts" (http://www.refdesk.com/)

A biography encyclopedia: http://www.biography.com/

❖ Searchable Library Catalogs

Libdex: http://www.libdex.com/

   (For this one, it's best to click on "geographical index").

Library of Congress searchable catalog: http://catalog.loc.gov/

❖ Directories

Switchboard (addresses & phone numbers—US plus Yellow Pages): http://www.switchboard.com/

Canada 411 (Canadian phone numbers & addresses): http://www.canada411.ca/

❖ Indexes

Ingenta (a general periodical index): http://www.ingenta.com/

ERIC (index to documents related to education and social issues): http://www.eric.ed.gov

For Further Study

Study Guide

1. What exactly is the Internet?
2. Define the following terms: browser, home page, URL, search engine, World Wide Web, document, link, bookmark.
3. What are "subject trees" on the Internet, and how can they help you?

4.   What are the key means by which you can evaluate the quality of information on Internet sites? Why is more evaluation required for Internet sites than for regularly published books and articles? Go to **http://www.lib.auburn.edu/evalweb.html** for more help in evaluating web sites.

Practice with the Internet

Try the same search on several search engines, e.g. Google, Vivisimo, Teoma, AlltheWeb. Why do some search engines come up with different results than others? Is it a correct assumption that google.com will most often produce better results than other search engines? [If you can't think of topics to search try the following: Skinner and behaviorism and walden; Lucrezia Borgia (or is it Lucretia Borgia?); Bill Gates and antitrust.]

Take the Internet Detective Tutorial:
(**http://www.sosig.ac.uk/desire/internet-detective.html**)

Assignment

Answer the following questions, using the search engine google.com, alltheweb.com, teoma.com or vivisimo.com. In each case indicate the keywords you searched with and URL(s) of the site(s) that had the answer:

     a.   It is believed that a European theologian, possibly Emil Brunner or Karl Barth, said that everything important he'd ever learned about theology came from the song "Jesus loves me this I know, for the Bible tells me so. "If you can verify that the statement was actually made, indicate what its wording was, who said it, and (if possible) under what circumstances it was originally spoken or written down. Note that some of the sites you find will not be particularly academic and may simply be parroting a rumor that is not accurate. Try to find a site that gives an authoritative answer.

     b.   The following is a real question asked by a librarian. Find the correct citation, including author, title, journal, volume number, date, and page numbers:

A professor here needs help clarifying a citation. He already has a photocopy of the article, but needs to know the volume, issue, and date in which the piece was published. The information we have is:
Author: Joachim Begrich
Title: Das priesterliche Heilsorakel
Journal: Zeitschrift fur die altestamentliche Wissenschaft (ZAW)

c.   In 1948, the Behaviourist psychologist wrote a novel entitled *Walden Two*. Find an Internet site for fans of the book and locate within that site an article about the book. What's the URL for the site and what's the title of the article?

d.   The following quotation is plagiarized from a source on the Internet. Identify the URL of the original source: "Jack the Ripper! Few names in history are as instantly recognizable. Fewer still evoke such vivid images: noisome courts and alleys, hansom cabs and gaslights, swirling fog, prostitutes decked out in the tawdriest of finery, the shrill cry of newsboys—and silent, cruel death personified in the cape-shrouded figure of a faceless prowler of the night, armed with a long knife and carrying a black Gladstone bag."

6

Other Resources You May Not Have Considered

Sometimes you get desperate. All the normal research avenues narrow down to footpaths and then disappear entirely. You're running out of time and you have nothing to show for the hours you've spent. Now there's a need for innovative action. This chapter will try to steer you in new and potentially fascinating directions.

Seeing Where You've Been

Before you launch into new sources for research data, it's probably a good idea to rehearse where you've been. Maybe you've missed some important resources. Let's use the following to go back over your research methods to this point and to check out possibilities that may have eluded you the first time you went through.

The Strategies We've Covered (Now for the First Time All in One Place)

❖ *Get a working knowledge of your topic* (You went to reference sources, including the Internet, and became familiar with the basics.) Ask yourself:

Did your reference sources suggest other related topics or give a bibliography that you've overlooked?

❖ *Assess the research topic, narrow it, come up with an analytical research question and suggest a preliminary outline:*

Did you set the topic so narrowly that there are insufficient resources? Or did you fail to set it narrowly enough and now you have a fuzzy view of what your topic is? Often the problem with finding relevant sources is that you are not focusing clearly on what the research project is setting out to do. You need to be able to express your research question or thesis in *one sentence* that deals with *one issue or problem you want to try to solve.*

❖ *Do a search in a library catalog, using controlled vocabularies and keywords as needed.*

Did you find everything that was there? If you began with a keyword search, you need to look closely at the catalog records you brought up. What controlled vocabulary subject headings were attached to the books you found? (Subject headings are located at the bottom of a catalog record for a book). If you started with subject headings, did you find all the relevant ones? Looking at the records you've brought up may help you to discover other possible subject headings. Did you consider books that might *contain* information relevant to you? E.g., for a paper on abortion, perhaps some key works in medical ethics might have relevant chapters on abortion.

❖ *Look at bibliographies or notes in the resources you did find. Consider separate subject bibliographies.*

Did you miss anything?

❖ *Do a search of periodical literature.*

Did you use the right periodical index for the topic?
Did you investigate the searching requirements for that index?
Did you choose narrow enough keywords or controlled vocabulary terms?
Are you sure you checked your library's periodical holdings carefully?

Let's consider some options you may not have thought of.

ERIC

One of the great untapped resources for research is ERIC. No, this is not a line-backer on a sophomore football team. ERIC stands for Educational Resources Information Center, a clearinghouse that makes available studies, reports, curriculum helps, etc. produced by educational institutions.

But don't think of it just as an educational database. Educators are concerned about virtually anything that might be related to education, from the effects of early poverty on adult job performance, to the ramifications of teen suicide. This means that a wide range of topics in the social sciences are covered, as well as quite a few areas of the humanities.

> ➤ Rather than have schools, colleges and universities put their studies on the issues affecting their work into filing cabinets, never to be seen again, the US government arranged to collect them and make them available to libraries. To do this, ERIC needed to have a two part approach:

> ➤ The reports themselves. They could be anything from a study of the effects of TV violence on high schoolers in Salem, Oregon, to an analysis of dyslexia in relation to reading speed in Podunk Junction. Such reports could be under 50 pages, though they might sometimes go to 100 pages or more. ERIC documents (i.e. these gathered reports) originally were microfiched, and each was assigned a number for identification purposes. Libraries purchased the ERIC documents and filed them by number. Now the more recent years of ERIC documents are available in PDF full text.

> ➤ A database with which to search the ERIC documents for topics of interest. Here the government had a stroke of genius—why not put the database on the Internet so that anyone can search it from anywhere? While would-be readers would still have to go to a library to find the documents they wanted, identification of these documents would be relatively easy.

One further bit of information—as ERIC developed, the database added a periodical index to journals in education. ERIC itself does not provide the articles in the periodical index portion but simply created the index as an additional feature. To distinguish ERIC Documents from ERIC Journals, the former were designated ED—so that each ERIC Document has a code number that looks like this: ED213562. ERIC Journals are designated EJ, as in: EJ498231.

Now we come to the part that drives a textbook writer wild—even as I am putting together this edition of *Research Strategies,* the US government has announced that it is consolidating the various subject clearinghouses that collected ERIC documents and is going to put ERIC under the control of a single contractor who will be charged with creating a new Internet interface and moving ERIC much more into an electronic full text environment. What this will look like is not exactly clear, but the final form is scheduled to be released in May 2004, too late for this edition (sigh). In order to keep you up to date, I will provide more current information for you at **http://www.acts.twu.ca/lbr/updates.htm.** (Thus you get your own private textbook website—cool!)

The most current interface for ERIC, now at **http://www.eric.ed.gov,** looks like this:

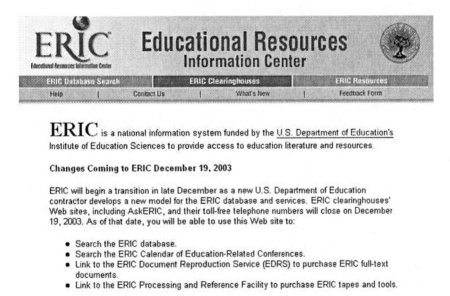

If you click on "ERIC Database Search," you can follow a thread through to basic and advanced searches. Your searches will get you citations to ERIC documents or educational journals indexed by ERIC, lesson plans, guides, even a question and answer service if you are stumped.

More recently, a number of periodical database providers have mounted ERIC, often including full text on recent ERIC Documents as an add on. Here's the EBSCO version of ERIC:

Clearly, a company like EBSCO knows how to enhance the basic product to make it much more searchable. Being able to limit on one screen by availability, ERIC number, the journal index or the ERIC document index, educational level, publication type, intended audience, government level, country of publication, and language, plus EBSCO's normal limiters, means that you will have excellent control over the one million + records in ERIC.

We don't have the upcoming free Internet ERIC interface to work with, so let's try a sample search using the EBSCO platform:

We can assume that teenage depression is a subject of interest to ERIC, since who of us were not depressed at some time during high school, and who of us didn't let our depression affect our schoolwork?

Let's begin with a keyword search, using the terms "teenage" and "Depression." Since teenagers are also referred to as "adolescents," we'll complicate the search somewhat by formulating the search as (**adolescents or teenagers**) **and depression**:

While there are a lot of results, meaning that we should likely put in some
more limiters (like limiting to ERIC documents), let's have a look at a few of
these citations as they are:

The first is an ERIC document with a code number that begins with ED. In this
database it is available electronically. If your library did not have access to electronic full text, it might have the same document in microfiche. The other two
citations are for ERIC Journals (with a code beginning with EJ) not available
directly from ERIC but accessible through your library's regular periodical
holdings. Of the two, one is available full text through one of EBSCO's other
databases.

ERIC has a "Thesaurus," a controlled vocabulary subject heading system. By
clicking on the Thesaurus tab, we can look up depression as a subject heading.
This may actually help to refine the search, because "depression" as a keyword
can refer to several different things, while "depression" as a psychological subject heading will have a specific meaning:

On this platform, I start by entering my term in the Browse box. First I move to
"advanced search" just in case I want to expand or limit my search. Then I

enter my term in the Browse box and hit the Browse button. That leads me to a list of relevant subject headings, one of which is Depression (Psychology):

Having clicked on the check box opposite "Depression (Psychology), I can now click on the Search box above to bring up all the records with that subject heading assigned. There are 3,000 results, obviously too many for what I want. Since I know I have the subject heading nailed, I can now click on the "Refine search" button to limit to "adolescents." While I'm at it, I'll also limit just to ERIC Documents rather than including the ERIC Journals, which are really a second category of index.

I now have 167 results, not bad for a database of this size:

Here's what the result list looks like:

EBSCO HOST   Research Databases   Basic Search   Advanced Search   Choose Databases   New Search | View Folder | Pr

Sign In to My EBSCOhost   Keyword | Publications | Thesaurus | Indexes | Library Holdings | Images

Searched: ERIC for DE "Depression (Psychology)" And adolescents and Journal or Document: ED   Add
Database Help

Find: DE "Depression (Psychology)"   in Default Fields   Search   Clear
and   adolescents   in Default Fields
and   in Default Fields
Search Tips

✓ Limiters set
Refine Search   Search History / Alerts   Results   To print, e-mail, or save an article or citation, add

◀ 1 to 10 (of 167) ▶ Pages: 1 2 3 4 5 ▶   Sort by : Date

1. Promoting Positive Mental and Emotional Health in Teens: Some Lessons from Research. American Teens. Child Trends Research Brief. Zaff, Jonathan F.; Calkins, Julia; Bridges, Lisa J.; Margie, Nancy Geyelin; Child Trends, Inc., Washington, DC., 2002 (ED469601)
Check for Availability   Full text from EDRS

2. Innoculating against Depression. Connect for Kids: Guidance for Grown-Ups. Louv, Richard; Benton Foundation, Washington, DC., 2002 (ED468481)
Check for Availability   Full text from EDRS

3. Multiple-Stage Screening for the Identification of Depression among Adolescents. Ettelson, Rebecca, Laurent, Jeff, 2002 (ED463480)
Check for Availability   Full text from EDRS

Don't ignore ERIC. It is a very good resource for many kinds of research. The fact that you can access its index on the Internet makes it all the more helpful. Once again, look for updated information on this database by going to http://www.acts.twu.ca/lbr/updates.htm.

Government Documents

Various governments produce vast hosts of information which is to be found in libraries, can be purchased, or can be found free on the Internet (depending on what the information is). Publications put out by governments cover potentially every area of life. The only problem is that they are *notoriously difficult to find.* If you are in a library that has government documents, rely on your reference librarian to guide you through the maze.

For US government information on the Internet, you can go to **http://www. access.gpo.gov/su_docs/fdlp/ec.** This site can help you find materials by agency or by topic. It can even guide you in finding documents in libraries. (In case the address goes out of date, the site name is FDLP Electronic Collection. Put that phrase with quotation marks into a Google search box, and the site should come up.)

If you are blessed enough to live in Canada, as I do, the Internet site you want is: **http://cgii.gc.ca/index-e.html**. The site is entitled "Canadian Government Information on the Internet."

For other country governments, try: **http://www.ipl.org/ref/RR/static/gov9000.html**.

Library Catalogs Other Than Your Own

There are times when you are sure there must be more out there than what you are finding in your local library collection. That's when other libraries can be a big help.

Some libraries are in consortium with others in a local area. They may offer a union catalog (one search will retrieve all relevant book titles) or they may offer a list of catalogs in the consortium so that you can search each separately. If there is a consortium, that should be your first avenue. Even if you don't have borrowing privileges at the other libraries, it may only require a trip across town to find the books you need and read them on site.

Your library may as well offer inter-library loans at a price or even free. In this case, you can search other catalogs available through the Internet and identify what you want. Two very good sources for lists of library catalogs on the net are:

http://lcweb.loc.gov/z3950/gateway.html#lc on the Library of Congress website, and the even larger site called LibDex: **http://www.libdex.com/**(Search by Country). Your library might also have a link to WorldCat, a resource that tells you what libraries hold a particular title.

Doctoral Dissertations

It sounds so intriguing, so right—if you want the best cutting edge research on a topic, why not locate a few doctoral dissertations? But the realities can be grim.

The searching tool for dissertations is *ProQuest Digital Dissertations*, a computerized index available in most larger libraries but few small ones. It's fully searchable and you can easily locate citations and summaries of doctoral work on your topic. ProQuest is now offering with its databases the full text of recent dissertations, but older ones are not yet available except by purchase through the ProQuest Internet website. Availability to dissertations has always been limited, because few libraries have extensive collections of dissertations. Here are some possibilities if you really want access to one:

➢ Find out whether or not it was also published as a regular book (some are). Note, however, that the title may have changed, so search as well by author in your own academic library or go further with one of the LibDex catalogs (see above).

➢ Find out if the title you want is available by inter-library loan.

➢ If you are feeling wealthy, you can go the purchase route by visiting **http://proquest.com/hp/Products/Dissertations.html.**

If you still can't locate a dissertation, you will probably be out of luck.

Full Text Reference Tools

There is a growing number of reference works that are also available in electronic format or which have an accompanying CD. Each library will have its own collection of such tools. If you are building your own library of reference sources, you may consider using a CD or even Internet-based subscription version rather than traditional print, as long as you follow this rule: *Electronic sources are best for reference information—short articles, graphs, pictorial data, etc. If your source is simply something you would read anyway from beginning to end, electronic searching of its text may be of little value to you.*

Happy researching with these tools. They can be a great help.

For Further Study

Study Guide

1. Summarize for yourself the research strategies covered so far.

2. What is ERIC, what kinds of documents does it provide access to, and what subject areas does it cover best?
3. Where do you find the index to ERIC? Where are the ERIC documents usually located, and in what formats do they come?
4. What is the Eric Thesaurus?
5. What's the difference between ED and EJ in ERIC?
6. What resources can provide a lot of help in locating government documents?
7. What is a "union catalog?"
8. What's the problem with locating doctoral dissertations? What avenues can you follow to get you hands on one if you want it?
9. Check with your local academic librarian to see what is becoming available in full text periodicals. Go to the following sites to see the current state of full text journals:
    http://www-us.ebsco.com/home/default.asp
    http://www.umi.com/proquest/

    For online books, check out:
    http://digital.library.upenn.edu/books/search.html
    http://www.ipl.org/div/books/
    http://www.questia.com/—a subscription-based library

Practice with other Resources

For ERIC, see the Assignment below. For some of the other resources listed in this chapter, try these searches:

1. From **http://www.access.gpo.gov/su_docs/fdlp/ec**, go to the link for "Locator Tools and Services."
    a. From GPA Access Resources, choose the topic "Social Programs," then find the "Social Welfare" link and go to the "Committee on Ways and Means." Find out what it's been doing in the current legislative session.
    b. Go to the link "Search the Federal Government" and enter the search "homelessness." Have a look at the resources there.

2. For Canadians, or those interested in Canadian things (and who isn't?), go to **http://cgii.gc.ca/index-e.html**.
    a. Click on "Federal Information," then choose "Space Information," locate the "Canadian Space Agency," and have a look at its information resources.

b. Click on "Municipal Information," choose "British Columbia," and find a set of pictures of my home town—Mission (when you see them, you'll wonder why everyone doesn't live here).

3. Go to **http://www.ipl.org/div/subject/browse/law20.40.00/** and find the constitution of Kazakhstan.

Assignment

Do a search for a topic relevant to ERIC using the Thesaurus function, adding at least one keyword to limit your search, and further limiting to ERIC Documents only. List at least 10 relevant documents that you retrieved in your search.

7

Case Studies in Research

It's all very well to read about the theory of research, but hands-on experience teaches us that we live in a complex world. Methods that may have worked perfectly well in one research project are disastrous in another. Keen minds and brave hearts are needed if we want to succeed in actually carrying out a research project. The moment you've been waiting for all along is here. Let's do some research!

"The Teenage Suicide Crisis"

It is a common fact that the rate of teenage suicides is increasing. For a sociology class, you've been given the above topic, and now you're amazed at the possibilities. Should you do:

> ➤ A statistical analysis of the prevalence of the problem?
> ➤ A study of why the rate is growing?
> ➤ An analysis of the social situations of those who commit suicide?
> ➤ A study of suicide prevention methods?
> ➤ Any one of a dozen other possibilities?

Before you go too much farther, it's best to get a working knowledge. Let's consider some reference tools, then move on to consider our approach:

❖ **Reference Sources.** After routing around the reference collection for awhile, I came across the *Gale Encyclopedia of Childhood and Adolescence*. While I thought this was a promising source, it has little on the suicide issue. So I turned to William Damon, ed. *Handbook of Child Psychology.* In volume 3 there is an interesting summary of the work of a researcher named Chandler who shows evidence that suicide can result from teenagers losing "persistent identity over time." He observes that "Even temporarily losing the narrative thread of one's personal persistence...leaves adolescents especially vulnerable to a range of self-destructive impulses against which others remain better insulated." In balance to this view, I sought out a few more reference articles and built my knowledge both of the prevalence and characteristics of the problem.

❖ **Topic Analysis.** Chandler's premise is intriguing. Could it be that teenage suicide is rising in prevalence because people's lives are becoming more disrupted through job displacement, family breakup, youth violence, fears for the future and so on? If so, and if Chandler is right, the relatively fragile self-identities of teenagers may be more threatened today than they once were. Every disruption is an attack upon personal identity, leading to self-destructive thinking.

But how do I formulate this into a proper research question? I can do so by trying to capture the essence of what I want to find out. How about something like this: *If Chandler is correct that adolescent suicide is linked to loss of persistent identity over time, can the increasingly disruptive nature of modern life be seen as a factor in the growth of suicides among teenagers?*

A preliminary outline might look like this:

> Introduction—The problem of a growing rate of teenage suicide
> I. Chandler's persistent identity model in relation to other possible models.
> II. Disruptive factors which might lead to self-destructive behavior.
> III. Analysis of increased life disruption among modern adolescents in light of the growing suicide rate.
> Conclusion: The value of Chandler's model in explaining the increase in teen suicides.

❖ **Book Search.** Here you have some options:

You could do a controlled vocabulary *Library of Congress Subject Heading* search under the heading: **Teenagers—Suicidal behavior.** That will get you a list of titles like: *Adolescent Suicide, The Cruelest Death,* and *Students at Risk.*

When you get down to reading them, you will have to look for references to Chandler's work or to themes similar to those of Chandler.

You could do a controlled vocabulary subject search, using Chandler's name as a *subject heading* to find any books written about him and/or his views.

You could get boldly adventurous and try a Boolean keyword search such as **Chandler AND suicide**. Here, you need to be careful. What kinds of keywords are being searched? Just title words? Titles and authors? All words in a catalog record? Depending on what keywords are being searched, you will find different resources. I tried this as a title keyword search and found nothing. Using a keyword search that covered the whole catalog record, I discovered two essays by Michael Chandler directly on the personal continuity issue. The search terms I used were found in the catalog record's contents descriptions for two books which were collections of essays: *Disorders and Dysfunctions of the Self,* and *Children, Youth and Suicide.* Without a Boolean keyword search, I probably would have missed these valuable sources.

You could do an author search for books by Michael Chandler. Trying this out, I could locate only one book, which was not on the topic of suicide (by the time you read this, he may have written a dozen, so please don't send cards and letters of correction).

❖ **Periodical Index Search.** Here, the first question might be: "What subject discipline are we dealing with?" It could be sociology or psychology or social psychology (life seldom fits neat categories, which is why librarians go bald). Let's suggest PsycINFO.

The first search should try to identify articles by Chandler on the topic (these are, therefore, primary sources, i.e. straight from the horse's mount, not that I'm calling Chandler a horse). Going with the "Authors" tab for the EBSCO interface of PsycINFO, you find his name and click on the check box:

EBSCO Research
HOST Databases | Basic Search | Advanced Search | Choose Databases |

Sign In to My EBSCOhost | Keyword | Publications | Thesaurus | Authors | Indexes | Library

Database: *Authors–PsycINFO 1887-Current*

Authors

Page: ▲▼   Browse for [   ] [Browse]

Select one or more items and click [Search]

☐ Chandler, Michael

☐ Chandler, Michael A.

☑ Chandler, Michael J.

Your search reveals:

1. Personal persistence, identity development, and suicide: A study of Native and non-Native North American adolescents. Chandler, Michael J.; Lalonde, Christopher E.; Sokol, Bryan W.; Monographs of the Society for Research in Child Development, Vol 68(2), Jun 2003. pp. vii-130. [Peer Reviewed Journal]
   References (202)
   Check for Availability Not at TWU ... Where can I get it? (Interlibrary Loan)

2. Continuities of selfhood in the face of radical developmental and cultural change. Chandler, Michael J.; Lalonde, Christopher E.; Sokol, Bryan W.; *In:* Nucci, Larry P. (Ed); Saxe, Geoffrey B. (Ed); 2000. Culture, thought, and development. Mahwah, NJ, US: Lawrence Erlbaum Associates, Publishers. pp. 65-84. [Chapter]
   Check TWU Library catalogue

3. Cultural continuity as a hedge against suicide in Canada's First Nations. Chandler, Michael J.; Lalonde, Christopher; Transcultural Psychiatry, Vol 35(2), 1998. pp. 191-219. [Journal Article]
   Times Cited (3)
   Check for Availability Not at TWU ... Where can I get it? (Interlibrary Loan)

4. False belief understanding goes to school: On the social-emotional consequences of coming early or late to a first theory of mind. Lalonde, Chris E.; Chandler, Michael J.; Cognition & Emotion, Vol 9 (2-3), Mar-May 1995. pp. 167-185. [Journal Article]
   Times Cited (31)
   Check for Availability Not at TWU ... Where can I get it? (Interlibrary Loan)

Notice one challenge with PsycINFO—It is not a full text index, so the only electronic full text you'll find is text linked from another EBSCO index. Still, this material—3 articles and a chapter of a book—are a great start.

Now, if you want to find articles about Chandler and his views on identity, try something simple—a keyword search on chandler and identity:

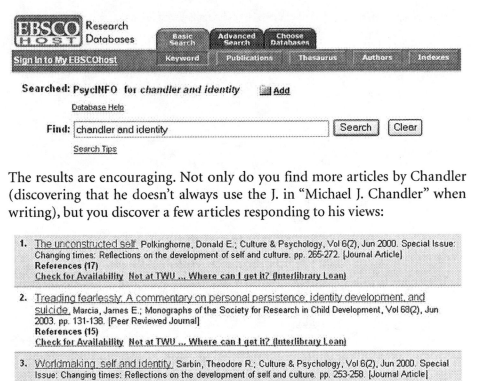

The results are encouraging. Not only do you find more articles by Chandler (discovering that he doesn't always use the J. in "Michael J. Chandler" when writing), but you discover a few articles responding to his views:

1. The unconstructed self. Polkinghorne, Donald E.; Culture & Psychology, Vol 6(2), Jun 2000. Special Issue: Changing times: Reflections on the development of self and culture. pp. 265-272. [Journal Article]
   References (17)
   Check for Availability Not at TWU ... Where can I get it? (Interlibrary Loan)

2. Treading fearlessly: A commentary on personal persistence, identity development, and suicide. Marcia, James E.; Monographs of the Society for Research in Child Development, Vol 68(2), Jun 2003. pp. 131-138. [Peer Reviewed Journal]
   References (15)
   Check for Availability Not at TWU ... Where can I get it? (Interlibrary Loan)

3. Worldmaking, self and identity. Sarbin, Theodore R.; Culture & Psychology, Vol 6(2), Jun 2000. Special Issue: Changing times: Reflections on the development of self and culture. pp. 253-258. [Journal Article]
   References (12)
   Check for Availability Not at TWU ... Where can I get it? (Interlibrary Loan)

Notice something in these results—You can click on a "references" link and get a list of all the materials the article cited. Thus, even if you don't have the original article, you can build bibliography by using the citation lists.

From this point, you could try searches like "suicide and identity," in order to find other views on the role of identity in suicide.

ERIC should be the kind of database ideally suited to a topic like this one. Let's go ask ERIC. A search of **Chandler and suicide** finds us only one citation—to an article already identified by PsycINFO. Let's try **adolescen* and suicide and identity**. If that doesn't work, you could search out some ERIC descriptors to see if there is some way to describe adolescent suicide rates better. In fact, a simple keyword search seems to work wonders:

Understanding Adolescent Suicide: A Psychosocial Interpretation of Developmental and
Contextual Factors. Portes, Pedro R.; Sandhu, Daya S.; Longwell-Grice, Robert; Adolescence, v37 n148
p805-14 Win 2002 (EJ660560)
📄 Linked Full Text

Social and Emotional Distress among American Indian and Alaska Native Students:
Research Findings. ERIC Digest. Clarke, Ardy SixKiller; ERIC Clearinghouse on Rural Education and
Small Schools, Charleston, WV., 2002 (ED459988)
📄 HTML Full Text   Full text from EDRS

Gay Youth: More Visible but Fewer Problems? Alexander, Christopher J.; Journal of Gay & Lesbian
Social Services, v11 n4 p113-17 2000 (EJ615927)
Check for Availability   Not at TWU ... Where can I get it? (Interlibrary Loan)

Models of Development: Understanding Risk in Adolescence. Graber, Julia A.; Brooks-Gunn,
Jeanne; Suicide and Life-Threatening Behavior, v25 suppl p18-25 1995 (EJ519409)
Check for Availability

Integration of Cultural Values in the Treatment of a Suicidal Adolescent. DiPilato, Marina, 1993
(ED370025)
Check for Availability   Full text from EDRS   Not at TWU ... Where can I get it? (Interlibrary Loan)

Two are ERIC documents and three are ERIC journals.

Where are you now? You've identified books and articles related to rates of adolescent suicide and particularly to Michael Chandler's work. Probably the only thing remaining would be to dig into the sources you've found to discover who else agrees with Chandler and to find out whether or not there are dissenting opinions. Clearly there is more than enough research being done out there to provide you with the resources you need. Your goal, remember, is to discover whether or not Chandler's theory is an adequate explanation of the growth in teen suicides.

Let's try one more, this time in the area of history:

"Lucrezia Borgia"

For a course on Renaissance History, you've been asked to write a research paper on a significant figure of the Renaissance period. For some strange reason, you think of the sinister femme fatale of the early 1500's, Lucrezia Borgia.

❖ **Reference Sources.** For a topic like this, any number of reference sources would do, even general encyclopedias like *Americana* or *Britannica*. There are also specific dictionaries and encyclopedias related to the history of Lucrezia's era. The *Britannica* entry provides good background and points out that Lucrezia (1480-1519) had a bad reputation for criminal activity, though it is possible that other family members were the real perpetrators (interesting!). She was a patron of the arts, etc. The *New Catholic Encyclopedia* has a good article on the Borgia family, something you will probably also have to study.

❖ **Topical Analysis.** While you could simply write a short biography of Lucrezia Borgia, true research demands more. The controversy over her supposed criminal and treacherous behavior would make a far better project. Why not focus on this research question: *Who was the real Lucrezia Borgia?*

A preliminary outline might look like this:

Introduction (to Lucrezia and her times)
    I. Her reputation for treachery.
    II. Possible evidence for her innocence.
Conclusion

Note that you will still have to relate Lucrezia's history, but now you are doing it around a definite focus.

❖ **Book search.** Because you are dealing with a person, the task of determining subject headings and keywords is significantly easier than it was with your last case study. Presumably, you can do a Library of Congress Subject Heading search under her name: **Borgia, Lucrezia,** though you may want as well to search for material on her relatives or even on the heading **Borgia Family.** If you find that these materials are limited in number, you might need to find books on Italian Renaissance history that will contain material on the Borgias.

You could also try a bibliography search using sources you have already located. One problem that may arise is that Lucrezia was Italian. Thus, many bibliography sources may be in a language you don't understand.

❖ **Periodical Literature.** Once again, the main challenge is choosing the right index to search. Why not try a broad based index like EBSCO Academic Search Premier (though your institution may have a different broad-based index like ProQuest or InfoTrac or FirstSearch)? No matter what index you use, you are going to discover that the results are limited and often mixed with book reviews and references to the opera based on her life. There just does not appear to be a great deal of periodical literature on her.

Still, reviews can lead you to key books on the subject and can provide a critique of those books.

Attempting to be brilliant, you decide at this point to do a lateral and try a Google search on "Lucrezia Borgia" bibliography. It does bring up some small bibliographies but minimal help with periodical literature.

This is an ideal point at which the advice of Chapter Three comes into play. When the normal tools cannot provide the answers you need, take the encyclopedia articles and books you already have and search their bibliographies. For this situation, bibliography searches will likely be your best option.

In the examples above, you probably hoped for easy and tidy results. Research isn't like that. Every project has its hazards and obstacles. There's nothing tidy about gathering information on a narrowed down topic. That's why we've looked at so many strategies. While you won't use them all in every research project, you need to have them in your arsenal just in case your next research adventure turns into a fight for your very life.

Who said libraries are boring?

For Further Study

Study Guide, Practice, and Assignment all in one

1. Go through each of the cases above and learn what you can.

2. Try out a few of these topics, narrowing them, then locating materials. Obviously you won't have time for a lot of in-depth work, but see what you can accomplish in an hour or two:

The Abortion Debate	Causes of World War One
Martin Luther	The Euthanasia Debate
Homelessness	The Crusades
Anti-Semitism	Confucianism
Moral Development of Children	Family Violence
Charlemagne Issues	Facing the Modern City

8
Learning How to Read for Research

It's all very well to amass an enormous bibliography and have all your sources scattered artfully on your desk. But if you're assuming that your essay or research report is now as good as written, you're a couple of sandwiches short of a picnic. Getting the research materials is only half the battle. Now you have to read them. This chapter majors on the tasks of reading and note-taking.

Reading for the Connoisseur and the Glutton

With a tantalizing heading like the one above, you may want to head for the nearest cafeteria. But read on—food for the mind is better than french fries.

Our generation is very big on what is commonly called "escapist fiction." This is the kind of book that makes no claim to be great literature with deep themes but does promise to take you out of yourself and into a far more exciting world.

I, like many librarians, enjoy reading adventure stories, spy novels and such. I've even been known to write and publish such fiction in my spare time. This does get me dubious glances from some people, but I am amazed at how many seemingly sophisticated academics read the same stuff.

The advantage of a thriller is that it lets you escape. You can sit back and let it happen without pondering or analyzing too deeply. Let the skilled thriller writer feed you the adventure until you scream for mercy. Escapist fiction is for gluttons.

I do not, however, call a well-crafted mystery novel "escapist" in the same sense. The writer of this kind of work dares you at every point not only to figure out who did it, but why and how whoever did it did it. In other words, such a writer does not want you to swallow the novel whole (as in a thriller) but to read it with discernment, pausing to think over clues with reserve and intelligence. The well-crafted mystery novel is for connoisseurs.

Where is all this leading? Simply to this basic statement: *Research is not for gluttons.*

Consider the problem you face: You have twenty-five scattered sources and seven websites waiting to be read. They comprise 3,423 pages in total. At an average rate of one page every two minutes, this will take you 6,846 minutes to read, or, in more familiar terms, 114.1 hours. If you skip classes for two weeks (or take a vacation from your job) and read 8.15 hours per day, you will have it all read. But wait a minute (even though you have none of these to spare)—I haven't allowed you the time you need to take notes on what you're reading. You'd better plan on three weeks.

Before I take you too far into the realm of the ridiculous, I think you can see that there is no way you will be able to read and take notes on 3,423 pages for one research project. The approach that works so well for devouring spy novels—gluttonously reading without much thought—is going to sink you when you try to read research materials. There has to be a way to pick and choose the best parts.

Let me show you the connoisseur's approach to reading:

❖   **Be Ruthless**

You may not like what I have to say now, but I do have to say it. *Any book you read for research purposes must be used and discarded as quickly as possible.* Forget that the author probably worked long into the night to produce the book, leaving a weeping spouse and children waiting outside the study door. Forget that for perhaps years the author was utterly consumed by the burden of this topic until it could be rendered into print.

You need information. The book you are reading has information. The problem is that it has too much information that is not relevant to your research topic. Thus you need to use every skill you have to sift quickly through the material you don't need and find the material you do need.

At this point I must warn you not to show this chapter to anyone with an academic title. Such a person may very well burn this book right in front of you. Professors are purists, and rightly so. They have written one or more theses for which they actually did read all 3,423 pages plus 74,689 more. They got into the hearts and souls of the authors they were reading.

You, on the other hand, are writing a paper that is due, along with two others, in seven days. *Be ruthless*. Read what you need and abandon the rest. It's your only hope.

One big note of caution: I am not urging you to read out of context. You have to read enough of an author's work to have a good idea of his or her main message. It is all very good to be efficient and discerning (the connoisseur) rather than a mindless sponge (the glutton), but be very sure you have grasped, not only what the author is saying, but why the author is saying it.

❖   **Get to Know the Material Without Reading It All**

No, this is not permission to do skimpy research. This is an attempt to show you how to zero in on what you need without missing anything important.

Here are the steps to take, first for books, then for articles:

Books

To start, have a good look at the title page, preface, foreword, and introduction. A book is not just a series of paragraphs. There is usually a motive and a plan, so the preliminary pages can often give you solid clues as to why the book was written and what it intends to do.

Title pages are often ignored because they seem to have so little information on them. But they can be important. Be sure to look at both the title and subtitle, since increasingly titles are there just to look cute, while the real purpose of the book is revealed in the subtitle. Consider these gems:

Lifestyle: Conversations with Members of the Unification Church

Passages: Predictable Crises of Adult Life

Sex in the Snow: Canadian Social Values at the End of the Millennium

The preface, foreword, or introduction will often tell you what the author is attempting to do in the book. There you can look for a theme, as well as for a description of the approach to the subject and of the material to be covered. Reading a good preface can sometimes give you all the clues you need to get into the really important data.

Second, check out the table of contents. This table forms the skeleton upon which the body is hung, the keystone that supports the building, the street signs that give meaning to the metropolis, the—

But why go on? The point is simply that the table of contents provides you with the basic structure of the book in its proper order. Here you find the good, the bad, and the useless. There was a time when tables of contents provided main headings, subdivisions, and even short paragraph summaries of the main arguments. Now chances are that most chapter headings you see will be cute but relatively uninformative. Still, it is worth your while to check out the table of contents. It may help you zero in on the chapter that you really want. And it gives you a sense of the writer's whole development of the topic.

Third, have a look at the index. Indexes can be good, atrocious, or nonexistent. Their real value (when present) lies in their ability to locate specific information when the book itself covers a broader topic. Comparing the indexing with the information in the table of contents can help you greatly by taking you right to the good parts of the book. But beware of two problems:

> ➢ Indexes often list many page numbers after each subject heading, forcing you to do a lot of looking up to find what you want. Comparing chapter headings with page numbers in the index might help you speed up the process by locating the most relevant sections.

> ➢ When you have located a subject through an index, watch out for your natural tendency to take information out of context. Remember that the paragraph you are reading on page 294 was preceded by the 293 pages that came before it.

Fourth, be sure to give the book a run-through, even if you are only going to use a part of it. If you fail to do so, you may miss completely the overall intent of the volume and thus misunderstand what you are reading in one portion of it. A run-through includes:

➤ Reading opening and concluding portions of each chapter to see what the author intended to cover and what he or she concluded.

➤ Considering the subheadings in the body of each chapter.

➤ Going over any summary or conclusion chapter at the end of the book.

➤ Possibly looking up a book review or two if the book is confusing or potentially controversial.

Fifth, when it comes to reading the appropriate portion(s) of the book, be a connoisseur of the argumentation, not a glutton who does not care what he is eating as long as he is eating. There is only one way to read when you are doing research—by asking constant questions. Questions are the absolutely most reliable key to good analysis. Ask yourself:

➤ What is the author saying?

➤ What point of view or background is the author coming from that might influence what is being said? Thus, what biases do you discern?

➤ Is the author really dealing with issues or are there some things missing or minimized in the argument?

➤ Is the evidence presented fairly? Is there enough evidence? Does the evidence support the author's case? Is there counter-evidence that needs to be considered before you automatically buy into the author's argument?

➤ How do this author's beliefs compare or contrast with other things you've been reading? (Here you should be able to group authors by what they believe so that you can see who supports whom and who opposes whom).

And so on. Don't merely absorb (gluttony). Analyze. Get involved. Ask probing and constant questions of everything you are reading. It will help your research immeasurably. What's more, your questions will help you start preparing your research for the final writing process.

Articles

With a periodical article, or an essay within a book, you lack some of the more familiar signposts—tables of contents, indexes, sometimes even subheadings in the text. To add to the problem, the writer may argue a complex point over several pages without stating a conclusion until the last moment. How do you get a grasp of the article's message in short order and make good use of it?

First, find an abstract (a summary of the article) if you can locate one quickly. The most generous periodicals actually provide their own abstracts in the text of their publications. If this is not the case for your article, the article may well be abstracted in a periodical index. With a good abstract, you can discern the author's main points and conclusion.

Second, watch for key propositions. *Key what???* A key proposition, despite its strange name, is a simple concept. It is *a statement of what the author believes to be true.* Whether or not it is actually true is something for you to discern, but it is what the author believes to be true. Most pieces of expository writing, whether books or periodical articles, have several key propositions dotted throughout with, hopefully, a big key proposition at the end of the article. There are two ways in which an author might present key propositions. Some authors start with a question, then present various lines of evidence, then state a key proposition:

Question ————▶ Evidence ————▶ Key Proposition

Others start with a key proposition, then present evidence for it, then re-state the proposition:

Key Proposition ————▶ Evidence ————▶ Restated Key Proposition

Your task, should you choose to accept it, is to identify how your author presents key propositions, then *find them.* Key propositions form the foundation or the skeleton of the article. Everything else is introduction or evidence. With the key propositions identified, you can get to the heart of what the author is trying to say.

[Note: The above procedure works just as well with books]

Third, check out the author's conclusion at the end of the article carefully. What is the author's bottom line? Presumably everything else in the article has some relation to that final statement of belief.

Fourth, if the article you are reading still gives you few clues, read the whole thing. There are times when you just have to muddle through, but it won't hurt as much as you think it will. As you go, try to abstract the article for yourself on paper. It will help your understanding, and if you ever have to refer to it again (in a week, by which time you've forgotten you ever read it), you'll be one step ahead.

A Final Word on Analytical Reading

We have been talking hard realities here—too little time and too much to read. Perhaps professors or employers one day will let students work on fewer but larger projects where they have the hours to do the job right. Until that happens, you will need to know how to practice discriminating reading.

Remember that books and periodical articles are sources of data. Develop those skills that will help you extract data with the greatest speed and efficiency. But beware of quoting an author out of context because you did not read enough to get the author's overall message.

Note Taking

We are all aware of those rare people who never take notes on the data they are discovering in research. Instead, they gather all their books and articles around themselves just before they start writing their first draft, then cite and quote their sources simply by hauling books out of the pile and looking up appropriate passages. Such people, of course, have photographic memories and the organizational skills of Noah loading the ark, or they are really only using one source for most of their data while occasionally referring to others to cover up the narrowness of their approach. Perhaps (heaven forbid), they're writing their research paper out of their heads and using the occasional book or article citation only as some sort of weak signal to the reader that they did some actual research.

For most of us, it's crucial as we read that we distill out the essential things we are going to have to include in our research paper. We don't have the minds or the stamina to retain everything, unaided by notes, at least not once our research goes beyond four or five sources.

Trying to teach someone how to take notes is almost like trying to teach a baby sparrow to fly. Most of what it takes comes from within you, not from instructions. I can try to help you by flapping my arms and showing you the motions, but you have to develop the will and skill to soar for yourself.

Generally I recommend taking notes from one source at a time, covering all of it. The alternative is to create pages with subject headings on them, then to record notes from various sources onto their proper subject pages. This latter method is not recommended, because it drags your notes out of their original contexts, thus losing the threads of thought of the authors you are reading. It's better to cover one book or article at a time, keeping all the notes for it in one place.

One of the biggest problems most students face is that they take too many notes that will later go unused. The key to this problem is to formulate and use a research question and preliminary outline as soon as possible in the research process. If you are one of those people who only discerns your outline for the first time while you are proof-reading the final copy of your paper, you have probably wasted a lot of time taking notes that ended up in the round file beside your desk. After all that needless effort, your paper is probably not very good anyway, because its structure was never planned.

Once you have a clear vision of what you want your research materials to tell you in dealing with your question, you next have to decide on a note-taking style.

❖ The Determined Photo-Copier

For some students, note taking is easy. Armed with fourteen dollars in dimes, or a charged up copier debit card, they simply photocopy or print everything that looks important, take all 140 copies home, and assemble an essay. Would that most of us could afford this method.

A bit of advice here:

➤ If you are using the copier or computer printer, make sure that you have recorded the *author, title, place of publication, publisher and date* for every book or article from which you've made copies or print-offs (*author, title, journal name, volume number, date and page numbers* for periodicals). You would be surprised at how many people I find wandering the library, wayward photocopy in hand, looking desperately for whatever source they took it from.

➤ Use a highlight pen on your copies or print-offs as soon as you have made them, while the information is still fresh in your mind. You want to mark the passages that were of the greatest importance to you so that you will not, sometime later, wonder why you made these copies and prints in the first place.

➤ Remember that you are at a disadvantage if you copy or print. "Me?" you grin. "I'm the one with fourteen dollars on my debit card. I'll have everything done in a tenth of the time it takes these longhand scribblers around here." Yes, but recognize that you have probably interacted with your material at a far more superficial level than have those "longhand scribblers." When you go home tonight and try to wade through all 140 print pages, you may find that you have entered a strange and cruel world in which no landmarks make sense to you and the reasons why you produced even half of the stuff totally escape you.

❖ The Note-Book Computer Whiz

With a notebook computer and a portable scanner like the C-Pen, you can input large amounts of material without ever photocopying any of it. Inputting is generally not much of a problem, but retrieval is. I regularly ask students what they do with the material they're entering into their computer. For many, all they do is print it and then make use of the notes in paper form. If this is the case, the computer is little more than a fast electronic pen.

There are some possibilities, however, for making far better use of notes created on your computer. If you can identify key words, you can use your word processor "Find" function to locate those words. You can open several windows of material at the same time and compare them right on screen. You can even buy a specialized student/scholar word processing system, which will allow you advanced file and search functions as well as helping you with the final paper and formatting your bibliography by whatever style manual you are using.

One word of caution: Because it is often so easy to input notes, you need to be careful that you keep your notes to a minimum. Simply putting everything you've been reading into your computer is probably counterproductive.

❖ **Hand-Typed or Handwritten Notes—The Quoter**

Some still prefer a low-tech approach or, lacking a portable scanner, they are using their own fingers to type material into their computer. At times they will want to get down information that is verbatim—direct quotations. There are some advantages to copying word for word, and (inevitably) some disadvantages.

Advantages

> You won't have to go back to the book or article later on if you need a suitable quotation. It will be right in your notes.

> A quotation method can give you greater accuracy, since you have the actual words of your sources. This is especially helpful when a topic is new to you. Even when you do not fully understand a writer's argument, you can copy a paragraph that states it. Later, when you are more in tune with the subject, the paragraph may make more sense. If you had tried merely to summarize it before you understood the topic, you may have misinterpreted the argument and carried that misinterpretation into your notes.

> The mere act of copying helps you get to know the material more intimately, since copying demands that you read the material more slowly and, in fact, that you read each word several times. In understanding, you will be far ahead of the photocopier when your notes are complete.

Disadvantages

> The process can become fairly laborious. It's easier to photocopy.

> You must be very careful to quote enough to catch the context. Alternatively, you could summarize the context in your notes, then copy directly the portion that is most important to you.

❖ Handwritten Notes—The Summarizer

This person reads a chunk of material, then summarizes it in his or her own words. The point is to condense several pages into a paragraph of notes or a paragraph into a sentence.

Advantages:

> ➤ This method is quicker than quoting.

> ➤ The process of summarizing forces you to think about the material and make it your own.

Disadvantages:

> ➤ The method does not work well if you are dealing with difficult material that is hard to condense.

> ➤ You will have to go back to your book or periodical if you find later that you need a quotation.

> ➤ You have to be very careful that you understand the things you are reading. If you misunderstand, you have no way of checking for accuracy later on, other than going back to your source material.

❖ Handwritten Notes—The Paraphraser

The difference between summarizing and paraphrasing is that the former condenses material while the latter rewrites each sentence in the reader's own words. With a paraphrase, you can expect that your paragraph of notes will be as long as the book's paragraph, if not longer.

Advantage:

> ➤ This method can be very helpful if you are working through difficult material. Sometimes just the task of rewriting each sentence in your own words makes the writer's meaning clear.

Disadvantages:

> ➢ While sometimes recommended by professors, this method leaves you particularly open to a charge of plagiarism (see the end of this chapter), since you are still reproducing the writer's work, thought for thought if not word for word.

> ➢ The method is laborious. Not only do you have to rephrase each sentence, but your notes will be as long as your original source, maybe longer.

Which Method is Best?

You can use any or all of these methods to advantage. May I suggest that you keep all of them in your toolkit, using each as it is appropriate, but for the most part avoiding paraphrasing except as an aid to personal understanding (even then, circle the paraphrase and label it as a paraphrase for future reference).

Further Notes on Note-Taking

❖ If you are quoting, use quotation marks in your notes. If the material you are reading turns a page in the middle of your quotation, put a slash mark or some other indicator into your notes to tell you where the page turned in the original. *Always* indicate, at the bottom of the quotation, the page number(s) of the original source you took the quotation from.

❖ If you are summarizing, conscientiously try to work at using your own wording. If you find that your wording is turning out like a clone of the original, then quote directly or photocopy. With summaries, indicate in the margin of the notes the book pages you are summarizing (in case you want to go back to the book later).

❖ If an insight comes to you as you are reading, include it in your notes. Put square brackets around it and end the statement of your insight with a dash and your initials, like this:

[Schwartzburg agrees with Smith on this point. I wonder what Flutnof has to say?—WB]

An "insight" is simply anything that occurs to you as you a reading, as, for example, the discovery that this writer agrees or disagrees with someone else, has omitted something, has made a statement that you would like to challenge, has given you a good idea you want to follow up, and so on.

❖ Make sure you leave nothing out of your notes. Give full information on author, title, place, publisher, date, volume number, page numbers, etc. You don't want to have to relocate a book or article you've already read. Chances are someone else will have it by now and you'll never find out what page that key quotation came from. Other than a cold shower, there's nothing as subduing as having to throw out perfectly good notes because you don't have enough information to use them in your bibliography.

A Gentle Warning About the Horrible Crime of Plagiarism

Just to end the chapter on a cheery note, let me caution you about the academic crime of *plagiarism*. Plagiarism, to put it simply, is passing on someone else's work as your own. The following examples, if they describe your actions, place you very obviously among the guilty. You are plagiarizing if you:

➤ Quote directly from a book or periodical without using quotation marks and a note to indicate that the material is not yours;

➤ Paraphrase an author, sentence by sentence, without acknowledging the author as the source of the material;

➤ Use, without acknowledgment, an idea put forward by an author when you can't find the same idea in two or more independent sources. (The point is that concepts that are unique to an author need to be acknowledged, while more generally used information does not).

Plagiarism is an academic crime because it is the theft of someone else's creativity, because it gives the impression that someone else's words or ideas are your own, and because most astute professors catch offenders quite easily (even those who buy their papers off the Internet), and then feel hurt that they have been lied to. This often results in a zero for the paper and, perhaps, further disciplinary action.

[If you are an international student, you may have come from an education system that saw the copying of published materials as not a serious problem because you were honoring great scholars. It is a serious problem for students in Western universities. For a handbook to guide you in every aspect of your academic life as an international student, see William Badke, *Beyond the Answer Sheet: Academic Success for International Students*. Lincoln, NE: iUniverse.com, 2003.]

For Further Study

Study Guide

1. What's the difference between connoisseur and glutton reading?
2. In what way do you need to "be ruthless?"
3. What are the four steps to discovering the overall message of a book quickly?
4. When you get to the fifth step (actually reading material you need), explain the best way to go about it.
5. What do "generous" periodical articles provide for you?
6. What are "key propositions" and how does finding them help the reading process?
7. What's the secret to avoiding the trap of taking too many notes that you will later not use?
8. What are some of the risks for those who take most of their notes by photocopying their sources?
9. What are the advantages and disadvantages of taking notes using the methods of quoting, summarizing and paraphrasing?
10. What are the 4 further instructions the author gives about key elements of note-taking?
11. Define plagiarism and explain why it is such a serious offence. You might want to supplement your knowledge with the following websites:
    http://www.csubak.edu/ssric/modules/other/plagiarism.htm
    http://www.hamilton.edu/academics/resource/wc/AvoidingPlagiarism.html

Practice/Assignment

1. How is your reading going? Is it efficient and effective? Go over the suggestions in the first part of this chapter and discover ways in which you can improve your research reading methods.
2. Assess your methods of note taking. Are they working for you? How would you improve them? Do you see ways to improve efficiency by using your computer in note taking?

9

Organizing Your Notes to Write your Paper

"I have seventy-five pages of notes, not counting the photocopy I left on the copier and the two pages which I think fell behind my desk. What a mess! How am I ever going to make an essay out of this chaos? Will there ever be meaning to my life?"

Yes, there will. Take heart. There is a way to organize your disastrous jumble or the chaos of notes in your computer, no matter how incomprehensible it now seems to be.

I hesitate whenever I suggest "my" method for note organization. What if your mind, heaven forbid, does not correspond with mine? What if I am totally out of touch with the logical categories you most enjoy?

Still, someone has to suggest something. Librarians, even though dull, are undoubtedly logical and thus better equipped than, say, Renaissance painters, to suggest methods of organizing information. I am giving you only one method (with some variations) because throwing too many methods at you can be confusing. If you don't like this approach, ask your favorite professor or another librarian to suggest a better one (I dare you).

My system can be called a "register method" of note organization. A "register" is an index list of some sort that enables you to organize data.

Consider an auto parts store. The parts are laid out in bins on row after row of shelves. The fact that the water system thermostats are next to the distributor

126

caps that are next to the spark plugs is not nearly as relevant as the fact that each bin has a number on it.

When I walk in and ask for a thermostat for a 1949 Wuzzly Roadster, the parts person does not immediately proceed to the shelves and start looking. He or she opens a parts book or searches with a computer to find the bin number for that model of thermostat. Then it's an easy task to find the bin with the right number on it and deliver my part to me.

Here's the point of the analogy: The rows of auto parts are your jumbled mess of notes. The bin numbers are codes you insert into these notes, such as page numbers and other symbols. The parts book or computer index represents an indexed outline by which you can retrieve your notes in a coherent way. This is how it works:

Your Notes

Some people write notes on 3 x 5 or 4 x 6 cards. This is, in my humble opinion, a grave error. Even an average-sized periodical article requires two or three cards, written on both sides to summarize its main points. A book could increase the number of cards to twenty or thirty. Not only is that costly, but you know you're going to lose a least a few cards before your research is done.

If God had meant us to write out notes on cards, he would not have allowed us to invent standard notepaper or computer printers that take standard paper sizes. Does not nature itself tell you that eyes, hands and pens were made for writing boldly on decent sized paper instead of scraping one-sixteenth inch high letters on miniscule cards? Are not computer printers set to standard size paper by default?

Save your note cards for the next part of my system if you wish, and produce your notes (if you are using print) on lined, punched, normal notepaper. Be sure, however, to follow the right method. As you begin notes on each book or article, be very certain that you include full bibliographical information in the notes (author, title, place, publisher, date, volume number, page numbers).

When you have completed your notes for a particular item (even if those notes are ten pages long), simply leave a few lines blank, then start notes on your next book or article, being sure again to enter full bibliographical information first. (If you are using a computer, see the alternatives below.)

One of the important things you need to do is *number the pages of your notes consecutively*. If you have fifty pages of notes on ten pages, then number your note pages from one to fifty. (If using a computer, see below). If you have photocopies, put them in the right places in your notes and number them too. Keep your notes in a binder so pages don't get lost.

Options for Notes Using a Computer

➢ Some people prefer to print their notes onto paper. In this case, the computer is just an input device, and notes are handled as above.

➢ If you are planning to use your notes in their electronic format, you need to determine how you want to set them up. Unless you have a note organization program, it's probably best to put all your notes into one file so that you can search them with only one search rather than several. The exception would be the situation in which the file gets beyond 40–50 pages. *Make sure you back up your information constantly if it's all in one file. You'd hate to lose the whole thing.*

➢ Your word processor's "find" function (in the "edit" menu) will become a retrieval tool, though in the organizing process you may need to input some codes (see below).

Your Bibliography

As you gather sources, you have to keep track of them, including enough bibliographical information so that you won't need to go on a desperate search for a lost date or volume number when you start writing your paper. Here's the minimal information needed:

◆ **Book**—Author, title, city of publication, publisher, date.

◆ **Periodical Article**—Author and title of article, journal title, volume number, date (e.g. January 1999 or Spring 2000), and page numbers where the article is found.

- **Periodical Article from an Electronic Periodical Database**—everything listed under **Periodical Article** above plus the date you accessed the article, and either the URL of the database (not of the article itself) or the name of the database, depending on what bibliographical style you are using.

- **Essay in a Book**—Author and title of article, title of book, editor of book, city of publication, publisher, date, and page numbers where the essay is found.

- **Reference Book Article**—Title of article, author if given (often abbreviation of author name is given at the end of the article), title of reference book, edition of reference book; and (sometimes) city of publication, publisher, date.

- **Internet Article**—Author (if given), title, publisher (if given), Internet address (URL), and date you accessed the information.

These days, the most practical way to compile a bibliography is with a computer file. That way, you can put everything in alphabetical order easily, and, if you have enough foresight, you can format your bibliography early on according to the style manual you are expected to use.

There are several bibliographical programs available that will enable you to store bibliographies in a variety of formats. The Pasteur Institute has a website that provides comprehensive description and evaluation of the best of them. See **http://www.pasteur.fr/infosci/biblio/formation-en/lobib.html**.

The low-tech alternative is to set up a card file. Each card would have full bibliographical information for only one entry in your bibliography. It should also indicate where notes on that item may be found. Who knows, you may remember that Octavius Flootsnoot said something about the issue you're dealing with. If you've cross-referenced your bibliography file to your notes, you need only look up "Flootsnoot," and your entry will tell you exactly where your notes for Flootsnoot are.

Your Subject Index

Note taking is easy. Retrieval is hard. The biggest problem most students face is that they've taken many pages of notes and photocopies, but now that they want to write the research paper, they can't retrieve the data they need.

Virtually anyone, even a seasoned author, gets writing anxiety—that moment when you are finally staring at a blank computer screen (with the cursor blinking in taunting fashion) or a piece of paper, and your mind tells you that this essay will never happen. You may have written brilliant works in the past (or not), but this one simply will never see the light of day. The fear value is tremendous. Now, imagine that you have the further problem that your notes are a mess, you're not sure you did enough research, and you can't find even the data you remember noting down. Writing anxiety now becomes a writing crisis.

The only way to save yourself all this angst, is to get organized before you write. Sure, I know you're thinking, *"My paper is due in 3 hours. I don't have time to get organized."*

My response is that *you don't have time NOT to get organized.*

Let me suggest a method that will break the back of writing anxiety and actually save you time in the long run. Here are the steps:

➢ Take a good-sized piece of paper and write your preliminary outline on it, leaving lots of space between each heading or subheading. (You **do** have a preliminary outline, don't you? If not, you've probably already wasted a lot of time researching things that aren't relevant to your topic, which is why your barely started paper is due in three hours.)

➢ Determine a symbol to represent each heading or subheading. These symbols could be the letters and numbers used in your outline (I., A., 1., a., etc.) or special symbols not normally used in written work: #, $ % + etc.

➢ If you are working in the medium of paper, read through your notes. Every time you discover data that is relevant to one of your headings in your outline, write the location (page number of notes) under that heading. In your notes, insert your symbol so that you can find the exact location of the data. (If this is confusing, see the example below.)

> ➢ If you are working with computer files, type the symbols (%, #. %, or whatever) into the spots in your notes that are relevant to your outline. The "find" function off "edit" in your word processing can then locate any symbol and its relevant notes any time you need them. Just remember to insert a space before and after the symbol so that the "find" function can actually find it.

Thus, with this exercise of organization, you cross-reference your notes with your outline so that you can retrieve the relevant notes as you write your paper. The outline may then look something like this:

The Limits of Behaviorism: *Walden Two* in Perspective

I.   An Introduction to Behaviorism

    # 4. 17 [page numbers only needed if your notes are in print; for computer files, only the symbol # is necessary].

II.   B.F. Skinner's *Walden Two*

    $ 3, 18, 3

III.   *Walden Two* as a Demonstration of the Limits of Behaviorism

    % 6, 12, 14-17

In the above, note that my symbols are #, $ and %. These symbols will also be inserted in the appropriate places in the printed notes or computer files for easy retrieval of data.

Why go to all this trouble? Simple. It saves time and alleviates writing anxiety. Consider the awful alternative: You begin writing the actual paper and get to heading number one: "An Introduction to Behaviorism." Now you have to do a keyword search with your find function (with unpredictable results) or rummage through all forty-seven pages of your printed notes, looking for material on this aspect. Having found your material and written this section of your paper, you come to your second roadblock: The second heading "B.F. Skinner's *Walden Two.*" Now you have to go through your notes again, for a second desperate search for relevant information. Then comes heading number three, and the whole nasty quest starts over again. In the process, you will have plowed through all your notes three times and recreated your writing anxiety three times.

Thus, setting up an index to your notes before you start writing saves you having to re-read your material every time you start a new section of your paper. Besides, you are left with a warm and comforting sense that you actually know where you are going before you start. When was the last time you had a feeling like that?

Indexing your Notes for Larger Assignments

There may well come a time when you are asked to produce a really large research paper like a thesis or dissertation. Now the process of note organization becomes crucial, because retrieval is much more complicated.

In general, the procedures outlined above work just as well on longer papers as they do on shorter ones. True, your outline itself may be several pages long, and you may have to modify what symbols you use to identify headings, but the same principle still operates—your goal is to cross-reference outline headings to your notes so that as you write the various parts of your paper you can retrieve the research data you need.

A few tips (beyond the obvious that you should always back up your files):

> Do your indexing as you are going along in your research rather than waiting to the end and being faced with the task of indexing massive computer files or dozens (even hundreds) of printed pages of notes.

> Make especially sure that you are keeping a good running file of your bibliography with full bibliographical information for each item in it. The larger the bibliography, the more the risk of losing things. Here a bibliographic software program may be a wise investment.

> If your preliminary outline should change as you are going, don't panic. Go back over what you've already indexed and transfer your old indexing, as best you can, to the new outline. Sometimes this will mean going back over your notes again and re-doing some of the indexing.

Research may be fun, but nobody said it was easy. Maybe the challenge is what makes it so much fun.

For Further Study

Study Guide

1. Write out an explanation of the "register method" of note organization, including a good description of each of the parts.
2. If note taking is easy, what is hard? Why?
3. In using a computer as your note taking device, what options do you have for retrieval?
4. Why go to all this trouble to organize notes and establish retrieval procedures?

Practice/Assignment

Assess your past method(s) of note organization. Would the register method work for you? Can you think of a method that would work better?

10

Tips on Research Writing

Research doesn't mean much if the presentation of your results is flawed. The kiss of death is to have a research paper returned with the comment: "Excellent bibliography, but your argument could have been developed more clearly."

Two problems stand out as the most serious: Getting your outline straight and writing persuasively. Let's deal with each in turn.

The Outline

Outlining is a major problem in any research presentation. If you are attempting (in fear, no doubt) a thesis or dissertation, the problem only compounds itself.

Let's visualize what we're dealing with first, then look at some possible solutions. The reason why the outline is so troublesome is that people receive information in sequence rather than absorbing all of the facts at the same time. Simply because a twenty page paper may take fifteen minutes to read means that some information must be presented before other information is given.

Let's look at it another way. Presenting an argument (that is, the statement of a response to your research question) is like building a house. You have to lay the foundation before you can move to the upper stories. Everything you build rests upon whatever you've already laid down.

Perhaps the best way to learn outlining technique is to look at specific steps and see these illustrated with specific examples.

Step One: The Research Question

As we have seen, the first step toward putting together even a preliminary outline is figuring out what issue you want to deal with. This involves narrowing your topic and stating a *single* research question. For our purposes, let's choose the topic of "Burnout in the Workplace." Our narrower focus will be "preventing burnout," and our research question is, "How can today's office worker resist burnout in the workplace?"

Step Two: Preliminary Outline Headings

Now you need to assess your question to determine what data you are going to need to answer it. For our example, presumably you'll need an introduction to burnout, explaining what it is and raising the issue that there must be means to resist it. You might, as well, assume that resisting this problem will involve recognizing the signs of burnout and taking some counter-measures to overcome those signs or to prevent them happening in the first place. Thus your preliminary outline has three possible headings already: Knowing the Signs of Approaching Burnout, Counter-measures, and An Introduction to the Problem of Burnout.

Step Three: Organizing the Headings

This is usually the hardest part. What you want is a logical order that is helpful to the reader. Above all, you want to avoid the impression that your paper lacks direction or that the direction it is taking is strange and hard to justify. A good outline should not be all that noticeable because your goal is to take the reader from introduction to conclusion as comfortably as possible.

Here are some tips:

➢ Get general and introductory matters out of the way first. Just as you needed a working knowledge of the topic when you started your research, you now need to give your reader a similar working knowledge, including

background information and a clear statement of the question you're dealing with. In the case of our burnout example, you would probably have to
define burnout, demonstrate what a problem it is, and raise the question
of what things could be done to resist burnout in the workplace.

➢ Look for a natural order to your headings, if you can find it. In our
burnout example, it seems more natural to discuss first the need to recognize the signs of burnout and *then* to consider possible counter-measures
to resist burnout (i.e. knowledge before action seems like a natural order).
Here are some other possibilities:

- In a historically-oriented paper (e.g. "The Early Conquests of
  Alexander the Great"), you might simply want to move the paper
  along chronologically.

- In an analysis of issues related to a topic, you can follow an ascending
  or climactic order, looking at smaller factors or arguments first, then
  moving up to the more crucial factors. Your last section could begin,
  "The most serious difficulty with_____, however,
  is_____." Ascending or climactic order adds power to a paper
  by leading the reader into increasing tension, much like an action
  movie builds to a climax. Resist giving away the most exciting parts of
  your paper early on—if you use up the good stuff early, you'll have little left to keep the reader interested in the rest of what you have to say.

- You need to include all relevant points of view on an issue, not just the
  one you support. When a research project ignores opposing arguments, the reader feels cheated, and the case you are making is weak-
  ened, not strengthened. An argument that pays no attention to other
  voices will not stand up to a challenge.

  If you are comparing or contrasting two or more viewpoints, there are
  basically two ways to go about it. Now's the time to get your wits about
  you, so go have some coffee or take a walk, then read on:

  If the two views you are discussing are relatively simple to explain and
  analyze, try a longitudinal method by which you discuss all aspects of
  view A and then moved on to discuss all aspects of view B. Suppose,
  for example, you were dealing with two views on the issue of

cloning—Go Ahead and Wait a Minute—What Do You Think You're Doing?
Your outline might look like this:

    I.   Introduction to Human Cloning
   II.   The Go Ahead Position
       A. All Science is Legitimate.
       B. We Can Trust Scientists Not To Put Us At Risk.
       C. The Benefits of Having Clones Outweigh The Risks.
  III. The Wait A Minute Position
       A. Is all Science Legitimate?
       B. Can We Trust Scientists Not To Put Us At Risk?
       C. Do The Benefits Outweigh The Risks?
  IV. Conclusion

You can see that we are presenting one position, then using our discussion of the second position to deal with the arguments against the first. Thus the Go Ahead Position will be described as objectively as possible. The analysis will come with The Wait a Minute Position.

But suppose that the arguments are getting complicated, and you're afraid your reader will have forgotten what the first position said about the legitimacy of science before you have time to discuss it in the second position. In a complex situation, you'll need a cross-sectional approach, which deals with both sides of each sub-topic in turn:

    I.   Introduction to Human Cloning
   II.   Is All Science Legitimate?
       A. Yes
       B. Maybe not
  III. Can We Trust The Scientists?
       A. Yes
       B. Not always
  IV. Do the Benefits of Having Clones Outweigh the Risks?
       A. Yes
       B. Maybe not
   V. Conclusion

Now you have the chance to deal with both sides of each issue in turn. By the time you get to your conclusion, your reader should have a cumulative understanding of the issues and of the reasons for your position.

➤ Avoid stringing out a list of 7 or more headings without subheadings, because this tends to damage the unity and coherence of your paper (just like leading someone down a winding path creates more confusion than leading the same person down a short city block with sights to see on all sides). How do you cover the ground without multiplying your outline headings? You do it by using fewer main headings and adding subheadings to them. Thus you *group* your points, arguments, etc. under 3 or 4 main categories and let subheadings pick up the detail. This makes a tighter structure that has more of a chance of achieving unity in the paper. See the outlines above for examples of useful ways to do this.

➤ Attempt objectivity at the beginning and do your analysis later. Here I need to get on a soapbox for a few moments:

Why does objectivity come before analysis? Because every view needs to be heard before you criticize it.

Suppose you are doing a paper on the well known (at least to me, since I created him) social scientist Horace Q. Blowhard, who has the audacity to argue that the death penalty should be instituted for traffic offenses in order to restore public order. Your paper, entitled "Why Don't You Stand In Front of *My* Car, Horace?" intends to rip the man to shreds. But how can you do this most effectively?

If you are still learning the fine points of intellectual maturity, you may want to begin you paper with the words, "Horace Q. Blowhard truly lives up to his name. If there were ever a reason for tar and feathers, Horace (no friend of yours or mine) would be it." From here, your outline would be:

    I.   Condemnation of Blowhard
    II. Some of the Most Vile of his Views
    III. Concluding condemnation.

But this is utterly the wrong approach. O ye contenders for justice and all it stands for, halt and listen up: *No one deserves to be torched verbally or in print before he or she has been given a fair and objective hearing.* Not even Horace Q. Blowhard.

I know what you're thinking now—When did true objectivity ever exist? All of us are subjective, so why not just state our views without worrying about truth and fairness to other viewpoints? Why try to give anyone an objective hearing? My answer is that, while this is not the time or place to get into the murky depths of Postmodernism, all of us know that it's possible to listen to someone, understand that person and treat that person's views fairly. Sure, our presuppositions will get in the way to some extent, but our goal still needs to be to understand the positions of others as best we can *before* we level either praise or crushing criticism. A good measure of objectivity is still possible for most of us.

Devastating attacks do not come before we have explained the position of our opponents. They come after, when both you and the reader have enough knowledge of the opposing position to determine whether you are launching the right missiles. Anything less than this is poor sportsmanship, bad form, bigotry, whatever you want to call it. Mature writing makes sure every view has been heard fairly before it is analyzed.

Some Tips on Research Writing

This is not a creative writing manual, but there are some things that you can do to give your paper the appearance of mature scholarship. Why do the research if your presentation looks like a dog's breakfast? So read on. There are certain rules of the game that you really need to learn.

❖ **Introduce Your Paper Well**

Introductions serve two purposes:

➢ They give you a chance to provide your reader with a working knowledge of your topic.

➢ They let you state your (*single*) research question. One thing to avoid here is the temptation to multiply your research questions along the lines of:

> "Why, then, did Skinner write *Walden Two*? Did he indeed believe that he could create Utopia with Behavioristic

methods? Was he blind to the problems in his approach?
Did he later change his mind?"

What you've done is create a shotgun blast heard around the world. You reader
has no idea what your real goal is because you have so many of them. The
paper itself will be as superficial and as scattered as your introduction.

Keep your introduction lean if not mean. Sometimes a real life illustration is
helpful to get the topic going. For example, if you are doing a paper on a historical figure, you might want to begin with an anecdote from that person's life
that typifies what you want to say about him/her. Beyond that, stick with the
purposes of an introduction—to provide a working knowledge and to state
your research question.

❖ **Always Describe Before You Analyze**

You thought I had long since fallen off my soapbox. Don't worry, I won't bring
it up again. But do it. Your writing will look more mature.

❖ **Avoid Ridicule**

When you disagree with a certain author or viewpoint, you need to maintain a
level of respect and decorum. Your opponent is not a "moron," "idiot," "stupid"
or "useless." (Believe it or not, I have seen all of these terms in student papers).
This kind of language reminds me of an elementary schoolyard with two kids
arguing about an issue until one of them runs out of ideas and says, "Oh yeah?
Well, I think you're stupid." Ridicule is the lowest form of argument. It reveals
immaturity and a lack of ability to address the issues in an intelligent manner.
Such language only reflects badly on you.

❖ **Be Logical**

By this, I mean that whenever you are traveling along a certain train of
thought, make sure your reader is in the caboose behind you. Don't flit
around. Don't jump to another track without warning. Always remember that
you are writing for someone who doesn't know where you're going. Lead your
reader along gently, step by step. Stay on track. For example, when you move
on to a new area of discussion, use a transitional phrase such as, "Turning to
the issue of…"

Having a clear sense of your research question and outline is a great help here. If you keep a single focus for your paper and understand the steps you need to take from question to solution, it's easier to help your reader stay with you. To make sure you're really on track, ask yourself for each paragraph in your paper:

> ➢ Is this paragraph in the right place in my paper (i.e. does it match the heading it's under)?

> ➢ Does this paragraph contribute to the solution for my research question?

There are times when I come across a research paper with a "bulge" in it. What's a bulge? It's a section of information that has little relationship to the paper topic. How did it get there? The researcher worked for a long time on something that, as it turned out, didn't really relate to the final paper. But no one wants to admit a big waste of time, so the researcher simply plugged the less-than-relevant material into the paper anyway. This turns what might have been a lean and mean research essay into an ugly project with an unsightly bulge in the middle of it. The poor reader is left to figure out what the bulge has to do with anything else.

❖ Be Explicit

I don't know how many students there are out there (good, otherwise intelligent, students) who believe in ESP. They assume that their professors can read their every thought even it is never expressed. Thus we get a gem that looks something like this:

> "In looking at the issues of Nicea, we must focus of the Arian Debate. The facts are well known and thus we move to the specific role of the famous Athansius in dealing with…"

What's a Nicea? What's an Arian Debate? Who's Athanasius and, if he's so famous, why have I never heard of him? If you don't explain yourself clearly throughout, your reader has no idea whether you know what you're writing about either.

❖ Aim for Clear Writing Rather than Erudition

The mark of an educated person is not the length of words and sentences used but *the ability to communicate complicated information in plain language.* Be concise. Say what you mean. Avoid like the plague every long word where a shorter word would work as well. Try never to be ambiguous.

❖ Watch Out for Flawed Arguments

These include:

> *Misrepresenting authorities.* If you are appealing to someone's work as support for your argument, be very sure that you represent that person accurately. Don't quote out of context, suppress information that would give a more honest picture, or anything similar. This sort of misrepresentation is best left to the tabloid newspapers.

> *Arguments from origins.* Just because an argument arose from a dubious source, it does not necessarily mean that viewpoint is wrong or right. If a nasty government that exploits the poor of its nation comes up with a wonderful invention to help end famine in the world, is the invention of no value simply because the government it came from is exploitive? Of course not. Those who know about such things are going to have to examine this invention and make their own assessment, regardless of its origin.

> Similarly, we can't always assess the value of an idea by considering the person who suggested it. While it might seem legitimate to doubt the advice on family unity put forward by someone who has been divorced seven times, you have to look at the person's material itself. The concepts may be sound even though the author does not exemplify them.

> *Arguments from Insufficient Evidence.* I am constantly amazed at the way some researchers skip over weighty problems without making their case. They use expressions like, "It is obvious that…" or "Such a view is unacceptable today…" when much more effort is needed to convince the reader that it really is obvious or unacceptable. My reaction when I see statements without sufficient evidence is to assume one of three things: the writer hasn't done enough research to discover that a controversy exists, or the writer has no evidence to offer and is trying to bluff through the problem, or the writer is bigoted enough to believe that his/her mere opinion is all any reader needs in order to be convinced.

How much evidence is sufficient? Enough to be convincing. When you write a research paper or report, you need to imagine a reader who is slightly hostile, who is not prepared to believe you. Then you must present sufficient support for your argument that your hostile reader will at least say, "Well, you make a good case." You don't need absolute proof, just enough evidence to get your reader to take your view seriously. If you don't have enough evidence to do this, then you will have to be a lot more humble about sharing your views. Admit that evidence is scarce and that, therefore, any position you are taking on the matter is tentative.

Sometimes, the evidence is not available at all. If that's the case, admit it. Write something like, "There continues to be much debate over this issue, and no consensus seems possible until more evidence is found." (Do not suicidally write: "I can't understand this issue, so I haven't made up my mind.")

❖ Know When to Quote and When Not to Quote

You should quote:

➢ When you want to back up your view with that of a prominent scholar who agrees with you.

➢ When something someone has written is catchy or memorable in its wording. For example, Walt Mueller, *Understanding Today's Youth Culture,* wrote this about how quickly some of today's teenagers resort to violence:

> "Playground and backyard conflicts are being settled in ways that would make Dirty Harry proud." (p. 130)

In one sentence, he evokes the nastiness of violence and makes his point that the violence is often modeled on that of movie heroes (though "Dirty Harry" is somewhat dated for people raised on Spiderman). A sharp quote can be gold in your essay.

You should not, however, quote:

➢ When you can say it just as well in your own words.

> ➤ When the material you want to quote is over 5 or 6 lines long (unless it is absolutely crucial in its original wording and is necessary for the central theme of your paper).
> ➤ When you already have a quote every page or two in your essay. You don't want to fill your paper with quotations. Your reader primarily wants your wisdom, not that of everyone else.

❖ **Know Some Basic Rules for Quotations**

Make it a habit to present your own material first, then *back it up* with a quotation. Quotations should not normally be used to present new data. Here the issue is one of authority. Every time you present new data with a quote, you are deferring to the authority of your source. That knocks the wind out of your own authority as an author. Let's put it this way: *Whose paper is it?* It's yours. Stand on your own two feet and make your own statements. Quotations are for backup and support.

Thus the pattern you should use is something like this: In your own words present some data or a viewpoint, then follow up with something like "As Joseph Schwartz has argued…", then quote from Schwartz in support of your data or viewpoint. Even if you are just presenting the views of someone (e.g. B.F. Skinner), present those views in your own words first, then follow up with a quotation from Skinner that summarizes his position well.

<u>Never, never, never, ever</u> write a paper that strings together long quotations interspersed with only a few lines of commentary by you. Such papers are doomed, since your professor knows that her ten-year-old could paste together the same quotations just as well. A research paper is supposed to be predominantly a presentation of material *in your own words*, showing that your can present data and use that data analytically to answer an important question. Use quotations sparingly, merely as support for what you are saying.

If you have a book or article that quotes another source, and you want to use that quotation, the rule is to find the original source that the quotation came from and quote that source directly. Until you go back to the original source, you can't know for sure whether the quotation was accurate or quoted in its proper context was. Only if you can't find the original source should you use the book or article in which you found the quotation. Even then, you need to indicate what you are doing:

3
Raymond Sludge, *The Red Rose,* 47, as quoted in Horace Roebuck, "Roses are Forever," *Flower Journal* 42 (May 2000): 76.

❖ Know the Uses of Footnotes/Endnotes/Citations

These days a lot of students are using short forms of citations (e.g. Jones, 241) instead of longer footnotes and endnotes. In this case, only the first of the purposes below is going to interest you. But don't forget that you can still add footnotes related to the other purposes below, even when you're using a short citation method.

The purposes of Footnotes/Endnotes/Citations include:

➢ Citing works you have quoted or borrowed ideas from. Most students are aware that direct quotations need to be noted/cited. But you need also to footnote borrowed ideas if they are relatively unique. Here's a (perhaps simplistic but helpful) rule of thumb: If you use an idea that you can only find in one or two of your sources, it's better to cite the source(s). If the material is found in three or more sources and you can't see that these are borrowing their idea from a single source in the past, don't bother with a note/citation.

➢ Stating further bibliography for the reader who may be interested in pursuing the matter. This procedure, which might look a bit tedious, shows the extent of your research and could earn you appreciation from the reader (and a higher grade if the reader is a professor). Even if you are using a short citation format in the body of your paper, you can still add further bibliography as a footnote.

➢ Citing sources that agree with your position. This is especially useful if you know you've gone out on a limb and you suspect your professor is ready to cut it off at the trunk. The support of five other scholars who agree with you may not prove your case, but at least it shows that you are not a flake. Begin this type of footnote/endnote with something like: "So too Steven Johnson, [etc.]" or "This position is also held by…"

➢ Defending a certain position against possible objections. Here you are not sure someone will object to what you are saying, but you see a potential flaw in the argument. It's better for you to point out the problem yourself and respond to it before your reader can raise it as an issue. A format for this could begin, "It might be objected that…but [then give your response to the possible objection]." This type of note shows your reader that you are not trying to present a whitewash with only your side represented. If, however, you find that the argument you are presenting is important for the whole thrust of your paper, include it in the actual text of your paper. Notes are for additional or less relevant material.

> Dealing with a related side issue that might spoil the flow of the essay itself if it were to appear in the text. This use is rare, but you may want to add to the depth of your paper in this way. Be careful, though, that you don't make the multiplying of notes a habit. I recently spoke with a world famous scholar who admitted to me that he has a problem with his use of notes. Only because I'm an overly polite librarian did I refrain from laughing. One of this scholar's most celebrated works was published as two equal length volumes. The first volume was the text of his book and the second was his endnotes. I'd say he has a serious problem (though his notes are often fascinating). Avoid having the same difficulty yourself.

❖ **Watch your Conclusions**

A good conclusion briefly summarizes the main focus of your paper and makes your final position clear. Avoid flowery, sentimental, or overly long conclusions. Say what you need to say and end it mercifully. In general, half a page at the end of a fifteen page paper is more than enough.

❖ **Give your Final Paper a Professional Look**

With today's computers, there's no excuse for a shabby final product. It should avoid typographical or spelling errors (use your spell-checker). Find out what style manual your institution is using, and follow it rigorously for title page, outline page, page format, bibliography, etc. With bibliographies, make sure you follow the format rules you've been given. If you haven't been given any, then choose a style manual and follow it (See **Appendix A** for more on style). Professors tend to assume that a sloppy product is evidence of a sloppy mind.

Research can be exciting, even fun. FUN??? Yes, as long as you see the path of discovery as an adventure. Research can be done well by virtually anyone, no matter what your initial ability may have been.

I trust that I have introduced you to sufficient strategies so that you can develop your skills to do first class work. The next stage is up to you.

For Further Study

Study Guide

1. What are the three steps to take in first establishing an outline?
2. In a research paper or report, what should you cover first?
3. Explain the longitudinal and cross-sectional approach to outlining discussion of more than one view on an issue. Try each method with the following outline elements:

Topic: Physician Assisted Suicide
The points of view: Seeing it as a beneficial aid to sufferers and Seeing it as wrong morally.
The subsections under each view—The problem of unbearable suffering, the wishes of the patient, the risk that we are playing God.

4. What are the two purposes of introductions?
5. Why describe before you analyse?
6. What are some things to remember if you want your paper/report to flow logically so that your reader can follow it?
7. What's a "bulge" in a paper or report?
8. What is the mark of an educated person?
9. Explain types of flawed argumentation.
10. When should you not use quotations? Do you agree with the author's position that your quotations should be few? Why or why not?
11. Why would you use "notes" in your research paper/report?
12. What should you avoid in a conclusion?

Practice/Assignment

Take a paper you have recently done and run it by the suggestions in this chapter. What should you change?

APPENDIX ONE

The Arrow Method for Terrific Research Papers

[The following was created for a seminar on research paper writing. It supplements the book *Research Strategies*, but in some cases overlaps with it. If you experience a small measure of déjà vu while reading the Appendix, be thankful that you've been given a chance to see an expansion, with enhanced examples, on essay preparation hints discussed in the body of this book.]

An arrow is a question looking for an answer. The answer is a target, but the secret to hitting that target truly is aiming the arrow properly. Given that your arrow has a point, a shaft, and a directional control (the feathers), it has the potential to find its answer as long as it is shot carefully.

Part One—The Point (The Research Question)

Why Most Research Papers Miss the Target

You have likely been trained to see a research paper as a way to force you to read a lot of material from many sources, then report on what you have read, covering whatever subject you have been given with as much depth as space will allow.

Thus, a research paper on the causes of World War I would begin with a brief history of the events leading to this war, then would list several causes, and would perhaps conclude with a statement that war is bad, and we should watch for warning signs so we can prevent war in the future. What would you say your research paper is about? *It is about the causes of World War I,* you reply, looking at me strangely. You read all about those causes in various books and magazines. You put that material together (that is, you synthesized it), and then you wrote a paper explaining the causes.

But your paper missed the target entirely. You see, a research paper is not supposed to be *about* anything. Please understand this. If you were writing a genuine research paper, and I asked you, "What is your paper about?" you should be able to answer, "It's about nothing." That response, of course, would result in some questions: *"What do you mean, 'It's about nothing?' Does this mean there's no a topic? Am I in an episode of Seinfeld?"*

Certainly, you have a topic. The problem is that my question, "What is your paper about?" is a bad question. It assumes that a research paper is intended to explain a certain topic, using resources that you have studied. That's a false assumption. Studying up on a topic and compiling data about it is not research at all.

What, then, is the point of a research paper?

A research paper seeks to use data from various resources to answer a question or solve a problem.

Data in this case is not an end in itself but a *means*, a *tool*. Research does not result merely in explanation of a topic. It is a problem-solving exercise that takes data from various sources and analyzes it to help you answer a burning question.

The Point and the Target

If you are merely reporting on what you have read, then you don't have to worry about the purpose of your paper. Your purpose is to explain to your reader everything you know about your topic.

But if you are in search of the answer to a question, you're not really interested in knowing everything about a topic, only what is relevant. Sure, you will do background study to make sure you understand the issues involved. But your data will become selective, because what you really need to know is *only that part of the data that can help you answer the question.*

EXAMPLE:

Instead of describing the causes of World War I, find a controversy that can become a research question. For example, it is often argued that the murder of Archduke Ferdinand was the chief cause of World War I. Your research very early tells you that this is an overly simple explanation. True, this particular assassination did lead to a series of events that began the War, but lots of people are murdered every year without the events turning into a war. Thus you become interested in answering a question like this one: *Why did the murder of Archduke Ferdinand become the flashpoint that led to WWI?*

There are several assumptions here to test out:

> ➢ This was no ordinary murder.
> ➢ The murder must have meant something more to the various sides than is apparent.
> ➢ There must have been a background to this particular murder so that the sides that created a war out of it knew immediately what the murder meant.

If an arrow is a question seeking an answer, and the target is that answer, then the *point* of the arrow is the focus upon which you formulate the question. Let's look at some arrows that will not fly, because the point is all wrong:

The arrow that does not exist:

This is the paper that has no question to direct it and thus no target to hit. Instead, the writer has assumed that simply explaining the subject matter of whatever the topic might be is enough. To the question, "What is the purpose of your paper?" the answer is, "I didn't know it had to have a purpose." Such a paper is doomed.

The blunt arrow:

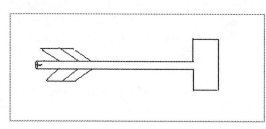

This arrow makes its point a broad, blunt rectangle by dealing with a broad issue rather than focusing on a narrow one. In our WWI example, this arrow would ask something like:

What were the events that led up to WWI?

With a question like that, it's not really clear what limits you want to set to your answer. You can detail all the events leading up the war, but you will simply end up with a survey that bounces off the target, not actually solving any problem or answering a real question.

The multi-pointed arrow:

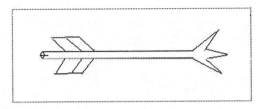

It looks strange and it flies strangely. The main problem is that this arrow seems to want to hit three areas of the target and will be fortunate even to stick to the target at all. Picture this research question:

I want to look at the causes of WWI and discuss why war is a great evil and show how WWI could have been avoided.

What is it that you want to answer here? I see three research projects pretending to be one. How are you going to unify them? Having three points of focus means you really have no focus at all. As you do your research you will find that your bibliography has to cover three times as much territory as it would if you only had one question. Your reader will be uncertain about your purpose, and chances are that none of your three questions will be answered with the depth they deserve.

The simply fuzzy arrow:

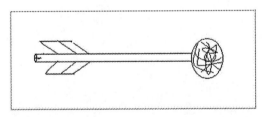

This arrow has a cloud instead of a point. It will likely float away before it ever reaches the target. This is a research question that doesn't appear to have any well-defined point at all. It might look something like this, if dealing with the causes of WWI:

What was going on with Ferdinand in August 1914 when he was shot and WWI began?

My question in response is, "What are you trying to accomplish with such a question?" It's not at all clear what your point is. Are you asking why he was important to the start of WWI or whether or not his assassination was his fault or what he did during August 1914 before he got shot? There's no way to research and write such a paper until its point is defined.

The never-will-fly arrow:

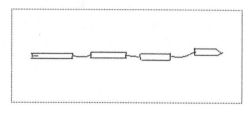

This arrow has a point, but any archer will tell you that it won't fly straight or reach the target, because it's built wrongly. It has a target to discover, but it's one of those questions that is built to fail, because its very formulation is all wrong. It has gaps in its shaft (replaced by wire) and no feathers. What does a question that's look like?

Would WWI have started if August 1914 never happened?

Or

How do the causes of WWI relate to modern international diplomacy?

The first is hypothetical, and the answer is "No one knows." Nor is there a good way to find evidence even for hypotheticals.

The second is a connection that you, the asker, have made between two things. Besides "modern international diplomacy" being impossibly broad, it is doubtful that modern diplomats ever even think about the causes of WWI.

Try not to sabotage yourself with a question that's flawed from the beginning and will never fly. Find something that:

> ➢ Can be answered with research data.
> ➢ Does not demand a wide diversity of research data in order to answer it (such as trying to find out what all of modern diplomacy of every nation does with the causes of WWI.)

> ➢ Does not involve hypotheticals and guessing.
> ➢ Does not connect things that normally are not connected.

The arrow that's already there:

This is a research question that's so easily answered that there is no research to do. For example:

What does Barbara Tuchman say were the causes of WWI?

Answer: Read her book, *The Guns of August.* If you wanted to turn this into a researchable question, you could ask:

How reliable is Barbara Tuchman's analysis of the causes of WWI?

Research Questions and Thesis Statements

We have looked at research questions, but some professors prefer you to use thesis statements. Put quite simply, a thesis statement is a proposed answer to a research question. It is not a conclusion as such (which demands that you've gone through all the evidence) but a proposal, like a hypothesis in a scientific experiment, that needs to be demonstrated.

For example, if your question is: *Are government sponsored programs or non-profit charitable programs better able to address the needs of homeless people in city cores?* the corresponding thesis statement might be: *Non-profit charitable programs are better able than government sponsored programs to address the needs of homeless people in city cores.*

If you are not comfortable with doing research papers, the research question approach is best, because with a thesis statement there is always a tendency to present the evidence that supports your thesis and ignore the evidence that doesn't. A more open-ended question tends to compel you to look at all sides. If you do take the thesis method, e.g. "The following paper will argue that…" you need to be very careful to look at the counter-arguments as well. You might, in fact, be shown to be wrong.

Types of Research Papers

Here are some common research paper types:

Descriptive Paper

This type of essay works at merely discovering and sharing information about something. It is not a true research paper but just a report on what you've read.

Analytical or Investigative Paper

This type of essay seeks to find out the truth about something. It often focuses on questions like Who? What? When? Where? Why? or How? For example:

- ➢ *Why is Osama bin Laden so opposed to the United States?*
- ➢ *When did the Reformation actually begin?*
- ➢ *What is the truth behind the legend of Robin Hood?*
- ➢ *How were the pyramids of Egypt constructed in a time when machinery was simple?*

Persuasive Paper

This type of essay takes a position on a particular issue, seeking to persuade the reader of the truth of something. There are two major types:

- ➢ Cause and Effect—Seeks to persuade you that something or someone was the cause or might be the cause of some event or situation. For example, consider these possible thesis statements:

  Support for abortion creates a slippery slope in which society loses its respect for life and other policies like euthanasia are allowed to flourish.

The reason why terrorism flourishes is that we have not paid sufficient attention to the problems of injustice in the world.

Note that cause and effect are notoriously difficult to demonstrate, because two events are often related only by coincidence. To show cause and effect, you have to demonstrate that the effect was caused by one factor out of all other possible factors. That's not easy to do.

➤ Contrast—Seeks to persuade you that one view is better than another on a certain topic. For example:

The problem of homelessness is best solved by local non-governmental initiatives rather than federal programs.

Assisted suicide should be condemned, not supported, as a means to end the suffering of the dying.

Practice with Research Questions

Determine whether or not each of the following the research questions is a good one. Then check the key below to see what I thought of the question:

1. *Martin Luther write anything criticizing the Jews?*

2. *What effect does homelessness have on the price of beds in Canada?*

3. *What's happening with Bill Gates now that he's made all that money?*

4. *Is there evidence that changes in emphasis in the _____ Child Welfare Program in the past 5 years are the result of pressure from the press?*

5. *What happened in Iraq in 2003?*

6. *How could the looting of the museums in Iraq in 2003 have been avoided?*

7. *What are the main features of Fetal Alcohol Syndrome and what can be done both to treat and prevent this condition? Should all alcohol containers carry a warning?*

8. *What are the ethical implications of human cloning?*

Suggested Key for Practice with Research Questions

1. **Bad Question:** Anyone with the works of Luther available can find the answer in less than half an hour. Thus the arrow is already in the target. A research question is more than discovery of a fact. It has to deal with an issue that can be analyzed in depth.

2. **Bad Question:** This question is the never-will-fly variety. Even if there is some connection between homelessness and the price of beds, there is no conceivable way for you to find out the nature and extent of the connection. Sometimes two ideas simply have no obvious connection or the connection is such that no amount of searching will help you find out what it is. A similar sort of question might be one like this: What has been the influence of liberal theology on morality in the United States? Presumably there could well be an influence, but I can think of no survey or statistical tool that would give you an answer. The key to avoiding these kinds of questions is to ask yourself—Is there a reasonable hope that I can gather evidence that will lead to an answer? If there seems to be no hope, drop the question.

3. **Bad Question:** The point is a cloudy fuzz, not a point at all. What are you trying to discover? What Bill Gates does with his day? Whether he's enjoying his money? Whether he should be spending it in other ways? As long as your question doesn't indicate a point or a direction you have no idea how to develop your paper. Here's a good focused research question to replace it: *How well has Bill Gates done proportionally to other young rich men in giving to charitable causes?* Now you know that your interest is going to be in investigating his charitable giving and that of his peers to see how well Bill's giving has gone. There's a point to it and evidence that can be found with a little effort.

4. **Good Question:** Why? It demands research and analysis and there is evidence available to support that research. You would need to discover when various complaints about the Ministry were prominent in the press, then see whether or not changes in the Ministry consistently followed periods of complaint.

5. **Bad Question:** This could be the blunt arrow where the point is not defined (i.e. what is it about Iraq in 2003 that you want to investigate?) or an arrow already in the target (answer = a war). In any case, I have no idea what direction to take this one. It must be defined better.

6. **Good Question:** In hindsight, it should be possible to look at what happened and show what protections could have been devised to prevent the

looting. Considerable writing has been done on the issue, so there should be lots of information.

7. **Bad Question:** This is your classic multi-pointer. With this many questions to answer, you will find that your project is cut up into a number of smaller projects and has no overall unity. Follow this rule—every research project must deal with only one issue.

8. **Somewhat Good Question:** There's a lot to research and analyze but you may well find that you run into far too many ethical implications to deal with. To solve this, limit your scope. For example, ask something like this: *In human cloning, what are the ethical implications for our definition of a 'human being'?*

Part Two—The Feathers (Outline as a Guidance System)

Most research papers that fail do so as a result of one of two reasons—lack of a good, well-focused research question or lack of a proper structure that can take that arrow right to the bull's-eye. In an arrow, the feathers do that job. In a research paper, this is done by the outline.

Why worry about an outline this early?

Many paper writers leave the outline to the end of the process. Some even write the paper then discern what the outline is so that it can be included on a contents page.

The real point at which outline construction needs to begin is once you have a research question.

> ➢ The points of your outline tell you what you need to cover and thus serve as a blueprint for your research. Your outline also keeps you from missing anything.

> ➢ The outline gives body to your research question, showing the direction that the arrow has to take to reach the target. As you are doing your research, you will begin visualizing the completed product, thus giving your paper more depth and substance. It takes time for a paper

to germinate in your thinking. The outline gives you a structure to allow that germination to develop properly.

➤ The very structure of a research paper is crucial to making the paper work. If you get things out of order, or if the order is not clear, it won't matter how much good information is there—the reader will see the paper as a failure. Thus, if you start thinking about structure and order early in the process, you are more likely to have the order right when you're done.

Steps to a Good Outline

Use Your Research Question

Your research question is the point of your essay. Embodied in it is the basic embryo of your outline and of the essay itself. Here's how to turn a research question into an outline:

First, have a good look at your question and ask yourself, "What am I trying to accomplish?" In a sentence or two, write out your purpose, giving your research question some body. Suppose your research question was:

Was the assassination of the Archduke Ferdinand as crucial a cause of WWI as is often asserted?

You could expand on it like this: There is a common view that the assassination of the Archduke created WWI. If that is true, then other circumstances will be much less significant. But if the assassination by itself would not have created this war, then the assassination may have been a final flashpoint in a more complicated process. What was that process?

Can you see how the question is leading to development of a structure?

Find the scope of your paper

With your analysis of your research question before you, ask yourself, What do I need to cover in order to answer my question? Look at the example above. You obviously will need to:

• Present and critique the common view that the assassination led to WWI

- Explain the events of that assassination and the reaction of the nations to it.
- Discover any possible larger issues of which the assassination was the final step.
- Consider all the evidence and come up with an answer to the research question.

You now have the elements of an outline. It may not be in the right order, and you may have to revise it, even add or subtract elements, but the basics are there.

Begin thinking about order

You don't need to make any final decisions yet, but these are some tips:

You will need an introduction that serves two purposes: to provide your reader with enough background information to be able to deal with your topic, and to declare your research question. Alternatively, you may want to formulate a thesis statement, which is an answer to your question, along the lines of, "The following paper will argue that…"

If there is any further development of background material that's more complex, it will have to go next as a separate section.

Often you will find that you are dealing with more than one point of view. Once you determine which point of view you are going to support, cover the view you do not support first, then cover the view you do support. Never reverse this order.

Think about your reader. What needs to be covered before something else makes sense?

Avoid stringing out your outline into 6, 7 or more points. A structure of 4 or 5 points works far better for the reader. Group things together so that you use fewer points, even if it means that each point has two or more sub-points.

Germinate

Memorize the outline you've created, even if it's still quite basic, and develop a habit of *germination*. What's "germination?" This is a hard thing to describe, but it's something like letting an embryo grow inside of you. Take time through your day to think about your outline—Would this order work better than that order? Have I left anything out? Have I included anything that really isn't relevant to my research question?

Then, as you gather your books, articles, and so on, and start to read them, begin to write your paper in your head, thinking constantly about your reader—At what points might my reader become confused? What would I change to make those points clearer? Am I being fair and complete by including all sides of an issue? Is my research question itself in need of some revision, and, if so, how will that change my outline?

By the time you write your paper, your outline should be working well for you, and your paper should be already written in your head.

Why do you need germination? Because depth and maturity in a research paper comes through working on it over time. Without this process, you simply have another one of those projects that are dashed off superficially and lack substance. Truly great writing needs germination. Your paper has to live and grow in you, or it will never have the power it should have for a reader. The way you allow it to grow is to build it around your ever-maturing outline.

Structure your final outline

Just as, with an arrow, there comes a time when the feathers are finally shaped and attached to the arrow, your germination process needs to come to an end, somewhere either just before the writing process begins, or during the writing. This final outline needs to be your roadmap for the final composition of your research paper, telling you at each point what you need to cover to develop your paper from introduction to conclusion. A paper written without an outline firmly before you or in your mind is a paper destined to confuse your reader and resist your hopes to communicate what you have discovered.

I cannot stress this strongly enough—your outline is the crucial element in hitting the target. An arrow, no matter how sharp the head or finely crafted the shaft, will not fly without the feathers.

So how do you go about structuring your final outline? If you have any doubts, follow a simple formula: Introduction, 3 or 4 points, Conclusion. KEEP IT

SIMPLE. If you find there is need for some complex discussion in point 2, then use sub points, like this:

Introduction
I.   The events of August 1914
   A. Early Part of the Month
   B. Assassination of the Archduke
      1. The plot
      2. The perpetrator
II. The common argument that the assassination started WWI
III. A reassessment of the cause of WWI
   A.
   B.
Conclusion

Practice with Outlines

For the following questions, create a 3 or 4 point outline, then compare your outline with mine in the suggested key (remember that outlines may vary):

1. To what can we attribute the fact that Martin Luther's attitude toward Jews grew more and more negative through his lifetime?

2. What is the best approach to reducing homelessness in an urban setting?

3. Is the virtual monopoly of Microsoft really as bad for the computing world as many critics say it is?

4. Is there evidence that changes in emphasis in the _____ Child Welfare Program in the past 5 years are the result of pressure from the press?

5. How could the looting of the museums in Iraq in 2003 have been avoided?

6. What is the best way to deal with non-violent teens in trouble with the law but afflicted with Fetal Alcohol Syndrome?

7. What are the implications of human cloning for our definition of a "person?"

8. Was the religious "conversion" of Roman Emperor Constantine genuine or a fraud carried out for political reasons?

Suggested Key for Practice with Outlines

1. Possible Outline:
Introduction [Explain who Luther was and ask the research question]
I.   Evidence of Luther's Growing Anti-Semitism
II. Possible Explanations
    A.
    B.
    C., etc.
Conclusion

2. Possible Outline:
Introduction [Explain the problem of urban homelessness and ask the research question]
I.   Current Approaches to Reducing Urban Homelessness.
    A.
    B.
    C., etc.
II. Critique of Such Approaches
    A.
    B.
    C.
III. A Proposed Best Approach
Conclusion

3. Possible Outline:
Introduction [Introduce the current monopoly issue and ask research question]
I.   Arguments that the Monopoly is Bad for the Computing World
II. Arguments that the Monopoly is Good for the Computing World
Conclusion

4. Possible Outline:
Introduction [Introduce the issue and ask the research question]
I.   The Nature of Changes in the Program over the Past 5 Years.
II. Instances of Coordination between Press Pressure and Changes
    A. Incident One

B. Incident Two

C. Incident Three, etc.

III. Possible Alternate Explanations for Timing of Changes

Conclusion

5. Possible Outline:

Introduction [Explain the problem and ask the research question]

I.   An Account of the Looting and the Failure to Prevent it

II. Possible Alternate Security Measures that Could have been Introduced

A.

B.

C. etc.

Conclusion [Take possible alternate measures and state an overall plan that might have worked]

6. Possible Outline:

Introduction [Explain problem of non-violent FAS offenders and ask research question]

I.   Common Current Approach[es] to the Problem

II. A Critique of Such Approach[es]

III. A Suggested Better Approach

Conclusion

7. Possible Outline:

Note that this is still quite an open-ended question allowing for many possibilities. Thus a variety of outlines are possible. Here's one.

Introduction [State the problem and ask the research question]

I.   Traditional Definitions of a Person

II. Elements of Cloning that Redefine "Person."

III. A New Definition of Personhood.

Conclusion

8. Possible Outline:

Introduction [Introduce Constantine and his conversion; ask research question]

I.   Evidence that the conversion was genuine.

II. Evidence that the conversion was a fraud with political motives

Conclusion

Part Three—The Shaft of the Arrow (Building the Substance of the Essay)

An arrow with point and feathers but no shaft isn't an arrow at all. In this section we will deal with the substance of this thing called a research essay. How is it put together? What are the crucial elements that make a mature, thoughtful paper?

Intent and Direction

The best research papers are characterized by a strong goal-orientation. This means that they have a purpose, defined by the research question, and a sense of movement from problem to solution.

A research essay is like the flight of an arrow from bow to target. When you aim the arrow, you see a target—a specific destination. You know that to hit the target you will have a launch, a period of travel through the air, and a conclusion when the arrow hits its mark.

But an arrow in flight is also subject to things like wind speed and wind direction. Similarly, a research essay does not ignore the influencing factors—context of the issue and the various options that could be answers to the question. There needs to be opportunity for recognition and analysis of other points of view, even opposing ones, as long as you make sure you stay on target with your main intention—to answer the research question.

Here's the rule: *Every part of your paper needs to contribute ultimately to answering your research question. There is no room for irrelevant details, even if they are interesting.*

Keep your paper goal-oriented. Don't allow it to wander or lose its sense of purpose.

Building the Paper

There are simple procedures that make the difference between a well-constructed paper and a mess. Here are some of them:

Use your outline like a blueprint.

Careful structure will contribute more to the success of your paper than anything else. *Follow the plan.*

You may be the sort of person who resists structure and organization in your writing, believing that structure limits your freedom of expression. But remember this: Structure is not for your benefit, but the benefit of your reader. The reader has a distinct disadvantage. He or she does not know where you are going in your paper. Without structure, much of what you have to say will remain a mystery to the reader. With structure, your reader is never lost. Beyond wanting to help the reader, you want to avoid leaving out anything that is important or including anything that is not important.

Carefully adhering to your outline as you write ensures that everything that needs to be in your paper is there.

Write out your outline and keep it (along with your research question) ever before you as you produce your paper.

Build your paper from the paragraph up.

While sentences are the basic building blocks of communication, paragraphs are the basic building blocks of an essay. Each paragraph advances your argument, like steps in a staircase. Think of your paragraphs as the smallest sub points of each point in your outline. Each has a topic and a unity that advances whatever you are covering in the particular element of your outline.

A paragraph is a collection of sentences that develop the same theme. Paragraphs may be as short as two sentences or as long as ten or more, but most paragraphs in a term paper will probably be between two and six sentences. If they are any longer, you should find a way to break them into smaller paragraphs.

We use paragraphs for several purposes:

> To introduce a new idea.
> To divide an idea into its parts in successive paragraphs.
> To give readers a break and make the essay easier to read. When I see a whole page without a paragraph break, I feel like it's an obstacle—too much text that needs to be read before I can take a breather from it. If that page is broken into paragraphs, I can pause in my reading when I want to.
> To help the reader to see more clearly where your thoughts are going. Every essay is like a journey through a subject. If there are no paragraphs, it is hard for the reader to understand the outline of the essay.

What are the parts of a paragraph?

> Topic Sentence—This is usually the first sentence, though it can sometimes be the second. This sentence tells you what the paragraph is about. It declares the theme or main message of the paragraph.
> Examples or further development intended to support the topic sentence—The sentences after the topic sentence should illustrate or support the message of the topic sentence.
> Conclusion—In many paragraphs, the final sentence will give the conclusion to the paragraph's idea.

When should I consider beginning a new paragraph?

> When you move to a new idea.
> When there is transition language, for example, words like "therefore," "turning to the issue of _____," "on the other hand," etc.
> When you have just concluded an idea and the next material is illustration or further explanation.
> When your paragraph is getting too long. Be careful here, however, that you don't break into a new paragraph part way through your idea.

Some tips for paragraphs:

> Always check to be sure that every sentence in your paragraph supports your topic sentence. Never have a paragraph like this:

There are too many people speeding on our freeways. My cousin has a new car, but he only drives it in town. He took me to a shopping mall the other day. We saw some of our friends there.

Notice that the sentences after the topic sentence have nothing to do with the topic sentence. Now look at this paragraph:

There are too many people speeding on our freeways. My cousin has a new car, but he refuses to drive it on the freeway, because he has been frightened by so many speeders. If we do not control the problem of speeding, a lot of people will avoid freeways, and more of those who use them will die.

➢ Make sure that each paragraph has a good relationship with the one before it and the one after it. Sometimes this means that you need to use transition words to help the reader understand where you are going, e.g. "Turning to the problem of…," "To illustrate this point, let us…," "The results of this policy, however, are…," "In conclusion…"

➢ Each paragraph must in some way support the main idea of the essay.

Make Proper Use of Sources

A research paper has some very definite features that make it different from an opinion piece or a sermon. First, it is an investigation of a problem, leading to a solution. This means that there is room for exhortation or application only in the conclusion, and even then the application should be brief.

Second, if a research paper is an investigation leading to a solution, it is a journey that requires the help of others, that is, the help of the books, articles, etc., that you gather during the research process. While you could simply follow a logical process of argumentation, leading to a conclusion, you need to recognize that no topic is truly original, even if your solution may be. Others have also dealt with the issue and have put forward evidence for their own interpretations. In fact, finding a solution to a research question most often involves weighing the conflicting interpretations of others and finding your answer as a result of your evaluation.

Using sources can be tricky. At one extreme, your paper could be primarily a set of quotations from books and articles, with brief commentary from you. At the other extreme, you could virtually ignore your sources and do most of the analysis yourself. The ideal is somewhere in between, where you use your sources extensively but still keep control over the analysis.

How do you achieve the ideal?

Group your sources by the particular issues they address, and especially by the particular viewpoints they support. Thus you should have a group of sources that deal with or support view A., a group that deal with or support view B., and so on.

Keep your quotations to a minimum, usually only one quotation for every page or two. Keep the quotations under 5 lines for the most part. Instead of quoting, refer. Use language like: *Smith has argued that Constantine embraced Christianity solely because he saw its power as a political force in the Roman Empire.* You are not quoting. You are referring to or describing a viewpoint in your own words. You'll still need to provide a note, but you'll avoid having your sources do all your speaking for you.

Recognize that the research paper is not supposed to be simply an account of what we already know but an analytical investigation of a problem. Thus, your own analysis, indeed your own presence, has to be seen in the paper. This means that you control your sources. They do not control you. It is you who must lay out the information that your sources provide, e.g. *Smith has argued that…Jones provides a contrary view…Green has added a new voice to the issue by asserting that…*[and so on]. You are using your sources to be sure, but you are controlling the process, building the shaft of the arrow yourself.

Almost never ever provide new information with a quotation. Use quotations to support a statement you have made first or to present a striking way in which an author has made a point.

Use sources that you agree with as well as sources you disagree with. A research paper needs to show evidence that you've investigated all relevant points of view and have treated your sources fairly. In general, even for writers with whom you disagree, explain what the source is saying before criticizing. Let your source be heard fairly before you evaluate it. Even when you do criticize, avoid language of ridicule. Make your criticisms logical and fair.

Avoid Theft of Other People's Work

Plagiarism is passing on the thoughts or words of someone else as if they were your own. It ranges from quoting others without acknowledging them to using other people's unique ideas as if they were your unique ideas.

It's relatively easy to avoid quoting a source without using quotation marks and a bibliographical note. It's a little more tricky, however, determining if you've stolen someone's ideas. A general rule of thumb is that, if an idea is found in two or three other sources which are not all dependent on one earlier source, you can safely use it without acknowledging its source. To be on the safe side, make a bibliographical note if a source is stating a point of view rather than just well known information.

There is another source of theft that is often not recognized—the use of paraphrases by which you take your source, sentence by sentence and simply rewrite each sentence using different words. In this case, you are not interpreting and explaining your source, but using your source's paragraph structure and thoughts in something that is very close to quoting. This too is plagiarism. Consider the following example:

Your friend says to you, *"I haven't eaten for a long time, so why don't we stop at McDonalds?"* Someone nearby says, *"What does he want?"* You explain, *"My friend is hungry and wants to stop for a burger."*

Notice that you did not paraphrase, as for example, *"My friend hasn't eaten for a long time and wants to stop at McDonalds."* You actually interpreted what your friend said and expressed it accurately but in your own words. The only word from your friend that you also used was "stop."

Here's an excerpt from an article that I published on the Internet on the significance of electronic documents. The original paragraph is:

Thus an electronic document disrupts the very meaning of the word "document." Electronically, a "document" can be viewed from anywhere in the world at the same time via the Internet, can have its wording and its look changed at will without any sign left behind that there was an earlier version, and can encompass other documents as well as encourage reading out of order. This may seem exciting (for example, we can hyperlink a document so that any possible problem or interest a reader may experience can be answered with the click of a mouse) but it carries dangers as well. ("Electronic Documents are Different," http://www.acts.twu.ca/lbr/electronicdocs.htm).

A paraphrase, which would *not* be acceptable, might read:
Therefore an electronic document upsets the actual meaning of the word "document." In electronic form, a "document" can be seen all over the world all at once via the Internet, can have its words and what it looks like altered at will without having left behind any indication that there was an earlier form, and can include other documents as well as support the idea of reading out of order. This might seem good, but it carries dangers as well.

Notice that I've borrowed sentence structure and even words from the original without really interpreting it. Now let me express the material in my own words:

Badke argues that electronic documents are radically different from other things called "document." Electronic documents can instantly be seen everywhere on the Internet, people can alter them so that we have no idea what the original was, they can be linked to other electronic documents, and the order in which you read them may not be important.

What I have done is to *interpret* what I've read and express it mostly in different words (though it's all right to use a few words from your source, maybe 5% or less). Remember, though, that the main point of a research essay is not simply to quote or interpret others, but to evaluate their work and provide your own arguments. Your analysis is extremely important.

Practice with Essay Structure

Let's walk through the development of a research paper around the following question:

Is there evidence that changes in emphasis in the _____ Child Welfare Program in the past 5 years are the result of pressure from the press?

Introduction [Introduce the issue and ask the research question]
I.   The Nature of Changes in the Program over the Past 5 Years.
II. Instances of Coordination between Press Pressure and Changes

A. Incident One
B. Incident Two
C. Incident Three, etc.
III. Possible Alternate Explanations for Timing of Changes
Conclusion

Here's a way we could develop our ideas:

Introduction

It is common for government departments to take press criticism seriously, even to adapt programs rather than have the press influence public opinion in a negative way. There have been many changes in the _____ Child Welfare Program over the past number of years, many of them appearing to be reactions to press criticism. Is there evidence that changes in emphasis in the _____ Child Welfare Program in the past 5 years are the result of pressure from the press?

I. The Nature of Changes in the Program over the Past 5 Years

Survey, with documentation, the major changes that have occurred, using chronological order as your organizing principle. By doing this, you are showing evidence that significant and frequent changes have been made.

II. Instances of Coordination between Press Pressure and Changes
    A. Incident One
    B. Incident Two
    C. Incident Three, etc.

Now take each instance of change and follow this kind of structure—Incident One: Prior press reaction, timing of change, determination of whether or not the change is a correction of the problem raised by the press.

III. Possible Alternate Explanations for Timing of Changes

Now provide analysis of any other possible driving motivations for the change. You have shown a correlation between press criticism and changes, but you have not demonstrated cause and effect until you've eliminated any other explanations.

Conclusion

In the conclusion, summarize briefly what you have covered, and make a final statement either supporting or rejecting the implication of your research question.

Part Four—Arrow Format (A Matter of Style)

Many faculty members place an emphasis upon papers being presented in a certain style. This has long been an issue with students, both because perfect style is so hard to achieve, and because it doesn't make much sense to give so much effort to something that really doesn't seem important to the construction of a research paper.

Style is important, however, for several reasons:

> ➢ The reader has fewer distractions away from content when the style (even proper title pages and tables of contents) is consistent and clear.
> ➢ The reader is better able to navigate a properly formatted paper.
> ➢ Adhering to style helps to guarantee that nothing important in the paper will be left out. This is particularly true in notes and bibliographies, where sloppy style can result in dates, volume numbers, pages, and publisher information being left out.
> ➢ Your professor wants proper style, and that makes style important in its own right (if, indeed, you're at all interested in getting good grades).

Style Software

These days, the pain of having to make sure every detail of your style has been checked and re-checked is gone. There are software packages that will help you format every part of your paper in proper style. I recommend one company in particular: StyleEase [http://www.styleease.com/]

StyleEase offers software packages for Chicago (Turabian), APA, and MLA formats. You choose the particular formatting features you need, and the program formats your pages as you go. Notes and bibliography simply require filling in a form, and the program then takes your information and formats it properly. While you still need to go over your results, the major task is done by the software.

(Note: This author has received no fee or benefit for endorsing this product. I just think it's useful).

Using style software is highly recommended.

For a great Internet site providing sample papers in a variety of formats, see http://www.dianahacker.com/resdoc/

So Where Are the Examples?

Did you ever, one day out of the blue, have a thought so revolutionary that it frightened you?

Earlier editions of this book had sets of sample pages from various styles along with examples for common types of bibliographical citations. Then it hit me—going on providing examples just perpetuates the false notion that any student can easily master bibliographic style simply by following some brief models. My experience, egged on by critics who kept saying I never provided enough examples, reinforced the fact that students aren't getting it—they aren't mastering style and likely never will unless they devote more time to style than content, thus hurting content.

So I've dropped the examples. If you want to avoid style software that can do most of the formatting work for you (and why would you?), there are still guides available. Go to the print edition of your style manual first, because it is more detailed. But if you want good basic information from the Net on the style your institution uses, check out one of the following sites:

APA
http://www.wooster.edu/psychology/apa-crib.html
http://webster.commnet.edu/apa/apa_index.htm
http://cal.bemidji.msus.edu/WRC/Handouts/APAFormat.html

MLA
http://www.hcc.hawaii.edu/education/hcc/library/mlahcc.html
http://owl.english.purdue.edu/handouts/research/r_mla.html
http://www.english.uiuc.edu/cws/wworkshop/MLA/bibliographymla.htm

Turabian (or Chicago)
http://www.libs.uga.edu/ref/turabian.html—Note with Turabian that both a footnote/endnote and a short note format are given. Ask your professor which is the preferred format for your school)
http://faculty.ucc.edu/egh-damerow/turabian.htm
http://libweb.bucknell.edu/Research_Tools/Citation_guides/turabian.pdf—a PDF file that requires Adobe reader to access it, but quite comprehensive.

Several Formats plus Sample Essays in Each Format
http://www.dianahacker.com/resdoc/—a terrific site for format issues!

For Electronic Items in your Bibliography—all 3 Formats Above:
http://owl.english.purdue.edu/handouts/research/r_docelectric.html
Beyond these, you should either purchase the full manual for your style or get some style formatting software.

Conclusion

Research papers do not have to be the painful experience many people make of them. There are some significant keys to making the writing process much easier than you think. We've seen a detailed explanation of them above, but let me summarize:

- ➢ Develop a well-focused analytical research question
- ➢ Structure your paper to answer the question
- ➢ Write intentionally, filling in the blanks in your outline with paragraphs that focus on your single goal, which is answering the research question.

978-0-595-31371-6
0-595-31371-X

Printed in the United States
67324LVS00003B/190-192